More Praise for *The Power of an Internal Franchise*

"Creative and empowering cultures that foster ownership are mission-critical in this new era of business. Companies that drive the entrepreneurial spirit will crush those that rely on outdated, top-down models. In *The Power of an Internal Franchise*, Marty O'Neill helps leaders architect and nurture winning cultures and prepares them for the challenges of the day. An important book for those looking to gain a competitive advantage and succeed in an increasingly complex and challenging environment."

—Josh Linkner, Chairman and Founder, ePrize,
and author of *Disciplined Dreaming*

"People make a company. Giving all employees the tools to be successful and help them meet a company's goal is inherently strategic. This book provides a great method for doing just that, and it helps frame how a company's leadership can think about integrating and informing every employee so that all involved—employees and the company—can reach their goals."

—Terri Thomas, CEO, BRTRC

"*The Power of an Internal Franchise* is a thorough, practical guide to implementing an effective entrepreneurial culture within any organization, regardless of mission, age, or size. The book also draws on, and assimilates in a comprehensive way, a substantial body of business, leadership, and related literature that can provide an additional depth of understanding for the curious or skeptical practitioner."

—Bruce Ballengee, CEO and Cofounder, Pariveda Solutions, Inc.

"*The Power of an Internal Franchise* will show you how to powerfully transform your business by turning it into a culturally adaptive, entrepreneurial workplace where the employees act like franchisees—in charge and ready to get results."

—Nick Morgan, President, Public Words Inc., and author of *Trust Me*

"Having a great business concept and a willing market are not enough—your people must execute your plan. Experienced entrepreneur and manager Martin O'Neill explains the Internal Franchise—defining your culture and empowering your people to make the franchise work."

—David J. Fink, PhD, Director of Entrepreneurial Services,
bwtech@UMBC Incubator and Accelerator

"Marty tackles a critical issue faced by all business owners—how to get the best out of your most important resources, your people. He advocates a culture that results in all employees realizing their role and stake in the growth of the company. This book provides actionable recommendations that will transform your workforce into an engaged, empowered group of stakeholders that drives growth for the company."

—Moira Mattingly, President, Summit Solutions

"I have built multiple successful companies by employing the techniques outlined in this book, so I am certain that if you follow the prescription for building an Internal Franchise, you too will realize the success and growth that occurs when everyone on your team begins thinking and acting like an owner!"

—Mark D. Gordon, President and COO, Odyssey Marine Exploration

"A work of art! The Internal Franchise is about building the future with step-by-step guidance, and Marty's higher purpose discovery methods do exactly that. This work will inspire and is a compelling message not to be missed by anyone in today's workforce."

—Maria Berdusco, President, Leadership International

"If you are looking for ways to grow your organization, *The Power of an Internal Franchise* is a must-read. O'Neill steps you through the process of setting up an organization empowered by entrepreneurs."

—Ray Schwemmer, CEO, CollabraSpace

"Prior to reading this book, I thought we were a well-run company that has stood the test of time. After reading *The Power of an Internal Franchise*, I realized we could offer our employees so much more and create a win-win experience for everyone. Just imagine what our businesses could achieve if we could create the entrepreneurial spirit in all of our employees. A must-read for all levels of supervision."

—Mark M. Reese, President, Schiff's Restaurant Service, Inc.

"An informed discussion of key elements of the Internal Franchise, including culture, model, leadership, trust, and rewards that apply from start-up to scale. Refreshing and principled insight for business leaders."

—Stewart Christ, CEO, Executive Peer Forum

The POWER of an Internal Franchise

Other Books by the Author

Building Business Value
How to Command a Premium Price
for Your Midsized Company

Act Like an Owner
Building an Ownership Culture
(with Robert M. Blonchek)

The POWER of an Internal Franchise

How Your Business Will Prosper When Your Employees Act Like Owners

Martin O'Neill

Third Bridge Press
Arnold, Maryland

Third Bridge Press
1290 Bay Dale Drive, #323
Arnold, MD 21012
www.thirdbridgepress.com

Ordering Information

Quantity sales. Special discounts are available on quantity purchases by corporations, associations, and others. For details, contact the "Special Sales Department" at the Third Bridge Press address above.

Individual sales. Third Bridge Press publications are available through most bookstores. They can also be ordered directly from Third Bridge Press at the address above.

Orders by US trade bookstores and wholesalers. Please contact Cardinal Publishers Group: Tel: (800) 296-0481; Fax: (317) 879-0872; www.cardinalpub.com.

Printed in the United States of America

Cataloguing-in-Publication data

 O'Neill, Martin F., 1959–
    The power of an internal franchise : how your business will prosper when your employees act like owners / Martin O'Neill.
       p. cm.
    Includes index.
    ISBN 978-0982056912
1. Employee motivation. 2. Leadership. 3. Success in business. 4 Supervision of employees. 5. Small business—United States—Growth. 6. Small business—United States—Management. 7. Organizational effectiveness. 8. Personnel management. I. Title.
HF5549.5 .O5 2011
658.3/124—dc22   2010939681

FIRST EDITION
16 15 14 13 12 11   10 9 8 7 6 5 4 3 2 1
Cover design: Bookwrights
Book design and composition: Beverly Butterfield, Girl of the West Productions
Editing: PeopleSpeak

To my mother and father,
who were always there to listen

CONTENTS

INTRODUCTION
The Last Untapped
Channel of Distribution

THE CHALLENGES COMPANIES face today are greater than any they have faced since the Great Depression. Without doing a great deal of analysis, we all feel that businesses need help. The government may have pumped $152 billion into the economy over the last couple of years, but money remains tight, unemployment is still high, and businesses need a new way of leveraging their current resources.[1]

Everyone in a company leadership role is looking to add to the top line and preserve the bottom line. The business model presented in this book grew out of years of building and operating companies and consulting to business leaders who were looking for ways to build better, more profitable companies. In this book, I'll present a business framework you can use to build a better top and bottom line. It captures the entrepreneurial spirit in all of us and can be used as a framework for responding to the ever-shifting business landscape. This framework is an "Internal Franchise."

Franchising is a method for marketing and distributing products and services. Companies like Dunkin' Donuts—which makes my favorite coffee—have used franchising to grow very rapidly and secure a significant share of their markets before competitors could catch up.

In a franchise system, a franchisor licenses a business formula—a complete way of doing business—to a franchisee. The franchisee agrees to operate the business according to specific guidelines and to pay the franchisor a percentage of sales as a royalty. The franchisor-franchisee relationship is governed by a franchise agreement, a binding legal agreement.

The franchise sector is one of the fastest-growing segments of our economy. Franchises employ more than 11 million people. The sector has outpaced construction, durable and nondurable goods, manufacturing, and financial services. In fact, a new franchise outlet opens every eight minutes in the United States.[2]

One reason for this success is that franchising provides the opportunity to run your own business with less risk than starting from scratch on your own. One of the hardest parts about starting a business from scratch is designing the business concept. In franchising, this step is already done for you. You simply have to learn to run the business. You have a serious head start on competitors who start from zero. That is why many Americans are turning to franchising to pursue their entrepreneurial dreams.

In an Internal Franchise, a company makes its operating model explicit and then franchises the operating model to its employees. The Internal Franchise is a framework for creating the ultimate channel of distribution for your products and services. The employees are then coached, mentored, and trained to operate the business at the highest level of proficiency. In an Internal Franchise, the franchise agreement is not a binding legal contract; it's the company's culture, an ownership culture.

An Internal Franchise addresses many of the fundamental challenges facing most workplaces today:

- Dealing with the lack of trust in society and in the workplace

- Understanding and providing for an employee base that wants opportunity and security

- Finding new markets for a company's products and services

Business leaders understand it is more difficult now to hire and retain an engaged, loyal workforce. They are looking for ways to motivate and inspire that next generation of leaders to innovate and take on additional responsibilities, and they are always trying to find new channels of distribution for their products and services.

If franchising is a method of marketing and distributing products and services, then an Internal Franchise is the *last untapped distribution channel for your products and services.* A channel of distribution is simply an avenue to move your products and services into the market. Creating this untapped channel forms a new energy in your organization and an opportunity to leapfrog your competitors.

> **If franchising is a method of marketing and distributing products and services, then an Internal Franchise is the *last untapped distribution channel for your products and services.***

Let's take a closer look at the three key components of an Internal Franchise: the operating model, the employee, and most importantly, the ownership culture.

The Operating Model

In a nutshell, an operating model is an organization's design for delivering utility to customers and earning a profit from that activity. It is the aggregate of these aspects of a company:

- The go-to market strategy
- The value proposition
- The structure and design
- The business processes

This is a long way of saying that what you do today is less important than *how* you do it.

For a lot of companies, their operating model is less a thoughtful process of leveraging the inherent advantages of the business and more a result of years of neglect. The design evolves over a period of time and is shaped by the personalities of the company's leaders and the fires currently being fought. You, as a leader, should decide proactively on your target markets and customers, your product and service offerings, your method of sales, your pricing strategy, and a host of other elements that make up the business design. Once you establish the design, you must then put it into action as an operating model.

An operating model is a company's way of doing business. Having a solid business design is not enough; you must have a workforce that can execute the design effectively.

Leaders who think hard about their company's operating model use a kind of "design thinking." As they design their business, they allow themselves to engage in a kind of divergent thought process. After they've explored all angles, they begin to hone in on the solution with a convergent thought process. Roger Martin, the dean of the University of Toronto's Rutman School of Management, calls this abductive thinking. In this type of thinking, the mind suggests a possibility and then explores it.[3]

Design thinking led the Four Seasons Hotels and Resorts to conduct a detailed study of its customers' attitudes toward the company. On the basis of the results, company leaders concluded that the Four Seasons could be a winner in the market by offering first-class service, but it would have to invest heavily in recruitment and training in order to have its service match its rhetoric. Making the decision to provide superior service wasn't enough. All the people in the organization had to understand the importance of customer service in the success of the business. They had to be motivated to provide top-notch service, be trained to serve customers, and be rewarded when they provided that service. First-class customer service had to become part of the Four Seasons operating model.[4]

An operating model like this manifests itself in the stories employees tell about what they do in their jobs. If you asked the leaders of the Four Seasons about their business design, they would mention customer service. If you asked employees about their jobs, they might say they are trained to identify a struggling customer and to immediately offer help. An operating model is only as good as the number of people who can live it every day!

The first step in building an Internal Franchise is to explicitly identify your operating model. To do that, you need to understand and challenge your fundamental assumptions about your business, your industry, and your customers and make explicit key business decisions about the customer, economic, and operational dimensions of your business. Next, devise procedures and systems to accomplish your business objectives. Once you choreograph the activities of everyone in your organization, you ensure they work together to achieve your business vision. Then, create reward systems to motivate the behaviors you need. You can teach everyone how your business works and how it makes money. You can reengineer your processes to ensure they produce the marketing result you want. You can define how your business works. In short, you ensure the policies, procedures, processes, and structures of your business work seamlessly together to achieve your business objectives.

The resulting operating model is what your employees will franchise. It doesn't matter if you are the manager of a major business unit of a Fortune 500 company or the leader of an entrepreneurial start-up. In today's business climate, everyone in your organization must understand your operating model.

The Employee

Engaged, entrepreneurial employees are the second major component of an Internal Franchise. Think about your hiring process. When you hire new employees, do you want technicians or entrepreneurs? Are you hiring people with specific skills, or are you hiring entrepreneurial people with an aptitude for the job they will perform?

I believe most people want the opportunity to act like an owner. But most people are never given the chance. Therefore, they are conditioned to think like a technician. They view themselves as a salesperson, an engineer, or a manager.

You need to begin to view your employees as entrepreneurs. And this starts with your hiring process. When you screen for attitude and cultural fit, look for people with entrepreneurial drive. Engage in open-ended questions that tap their background, demonstrate their ability to understand customer needs, and illustrate how they have served customers in the past. When you begin to explain to prospective employees that they will be given the opportunity to act like an owner, the entrepreneur in them will awaken. Then, when they join your company and begin to live in an ownership culture, their entrepreneurial spirit will grow. They will begin to act like stewards of the business and, in the best of cases, act like owners of your business. Your ownership culture becomes a brand that nurtures loyalty between your employees and your company or organization.

Your job as a leader is to attract and grow entrepreneurs, or "intrapreneurs," who can franchise your operating model and execute it at a high level of proficiency. You must attract people with a positive, entrepreneurial attitude and then create an environment that nurtures and supports an entrepreneurial spirit and creates the behaviors you need. That's where an ownership culture comes into play. It's your franchise agreement.

The Ownership Culture

A franchise agreement is a legal document that sets limits on the activities of the franchisee. Its purpose is to enforce the principle that what's good for the system is good for the franchisee. The franchise agreement aligns everyone's behaviors with the overall goals of the franchise system; then, both the system and the individual operators will benefit.

Likewise, a corporate culture enforces shared principles and values and establishes accepted behavior for all members of the organization. An ownership culture compels everyone to think and act like an owner of the business. An ownership culture enforces the Law of the Entrepreneur:

> What's good for the business is good for the entrepreneur, and what's good for the entrepreneur is good for the business.

An ownership culture is a bond that is cast in trust among the constituent members of the organization. This strong, empowered culture implies that people will act with the best interest of the company in mind. It creates an environment where all the people in the organization feel like they own their franchised operation and act accordingly. Therefore, an ownership culture is the franchise agreement in an Internal Franchise.

Putting an Internal Franchise to Work

This book covers every element of the Internal Franchise from every direction. You'll understand how an Internal Franchise can transform your organization. You will explore culture's role as the franchise agreement in your Internal Franchise and the power of branding your workplace. You will also understand what a corporate culture is, how to identify it, why it's important, and what its role is in aligning people with your business goals. You'll then review research findings that describe the link between corporate culture and business performance and learn how a strong, empowered culture is the corporate culture of choice. In addition, you will learn how to identify the principles and values that are at the foundation of your organization and how an Internal Franchise can brand your workplace and help you attract, motivate, and retain the people you need.

Next, I will lead you through the process of specifying your operating model. Here, you will explicitly define your vision for your business or business segment. You will have the opportunity to explore your business focus, economic model, operating parameters, and core processes. When you understand these components, you can devise effective business processes, procedures, structures, and systems that ensure your vision is fulfilled. More importantly, the process of crystallizing your operating model is a consensus-building process. It allows you to solicit and consider the input of everyone in your organization. It prepares you to teach everyone how the business works. An operating model is not a strategic plan or even a business plan; it's a tool for building consensus on the direction of the business and for teaching everyone in the organization what the business is for, how it works, and what everyone needs to do to make sure it is successful.

Then, we will look at the key characteristics we value most in the people with whom we work. We can create the most unique operating model around, but it will produce value only when it is executed by highly talented and motivated people. This book will demonstrate that what most of us are actually seeking in our employees is embodied in the spirit and characteristics of the entrepreneur.

Finally, we will look at motivating your entrepreneurial workforce and sustaining momentum for years to come. This will include a discussion of how leaders should reward entrepreneurial employees, how the outward signs of an Internal Franchise positively shape the workforce, and the best practices on leading an Internal Franchise.

1

Unleashing the Power of an Internal Franchise

ANYONE WHO HAS worked in an organization or business that embraces the entrepreneurial spirit knows how exhilarating it is. There is a buzz in the air. The action on the shop floor and in the hallways is so intense that coming out of an office is like merging into rush-hour traffic on an interstate highway. Decisions are made on the fly without the need for formal meetings or approvals. The esprit de corps is palpable. The whole team pitches in to do what it takes to succeed. Competitive energy resonates around the clock. Everyone in the organization focuses on winning and satisfying new customers. A sense of purpose dominates the environment. Entrepreneurial spirit is alive.

When entrepreneurial spirit permeates every corner of an organization, the entrepreneur lurking in each of us awakens. Think about what characterizes a successful entrepreneur. She has tremendous belief in her abilities and in her vision for the business. Perhaps she developed a way of operating that allows her to earn a profit. Maybe she is prone to action and doesn't worry about making mistakes. Instead, she learns from her mistakes. She understands that when the business succeeds, she'll succeed, so she focuses her energy on building a successful business.

Now, imagine that every person in your organization shares these same beliefs. How powerful! Imagine the possibilities if everyone in your organization believes in the purpose of your business. Imagine the possibilities if everyone in your organization believes in the reward for exercising initiative in creating value for your customers and profit for your business. Just imagine the possibilities!

When everyone in the business knows how the company operates and how the company makes money, and when they understand that as the company is rewarded, so will they be, you'll see the power of the Internal Franchise. The possibilities are endless. The impact is immediate.

Immediate Impact

First, you will notice that your people interact in positive ways. The focus is on winning new customers, not on internal politics. People help each other. Employees keep the best interest of your business in mind because it's in their own best interest. They are accountable for business results. Nobody says, "That's not my job." Everyone pitches in whenever needed, doing whatever it takes to build a successful business.

You can also expect business performance to improve. In an Internal Franchise, everyone understands how the company or business unit makes money. Because employees focus on the customer and the market, they identify new business opportunities. When they understand the value drivers of the business and their success is tied to the success of the business, they control costs better. They have a line of sight between their daily activities and the income statement, balance sheet, or operating budget. Everyone looks for ways to incrementally improve the business so the business can become more successful.

Your company will attract and retain top talent because an Internal Franchise provides career security for everyone in the organization. Employees find their jobs much more fulfilling because they are provided with a broad view of how the business works. Their level of responsibility and authority increases. As a result, they become more valuable to you and to the employment market in general. Even if your company goes out of business tomorrow or is restructured, acquired, or sold, your employees are secure because their skills and experience are in demand. They would never think of going to work for an organization that simply views them as a pair of hands. They are going to stay where they are.

Sound too good to be true? These results are not only possible but also likely when you develop all the components that comprise an Internal Franchise. Here are a couple of my favorite stories that illustrate the power of an Internal Franchise.

Bankruptcy Can Be Humbling

Pierre Foods in Cincinnati, Ohio, produces a broad line of fully cooked beef, pork, chicken, turkey, peanut butter, and bakery products for school, food-service, retail, vending, and convenience-store markets. The CEO of this $600 million company is Bill Toler, a leader who cut his teeth with large companies like Procter and Gamble and Nabisco, as well as a venture-backed Internet start-up. One of the challenges Toler had when he grabbed the wheel at Pierre in January 2009 was clarifying the context in which Pierre Foods operated (big) versus the content of how it operated (midmarket). In other words, the leadership team at Pierre had to buy into a new operating model that balanced where they wanted to be with the reality that faced them every day. This was especially challenging because the company filed for bankruptcy in June 2008.[1] But it was this emotional, catalytic event that shocked the organization into changes that aligned culture, incentives, and business objectives. Pierre began to work hard to replicate the positive attributes of its culture in each of its plants. Bill Toler continued to build and incentivize his leadership team by aligning the incentive program to business results. As a result of many of these changes, CEO Bill Toler continues to build a valuable, profitable company.

An Expectation Framework

Another example of the power of an Internal Franchise involves Bruce Ballengee, the CEO of Pariveda Solutions of Dallas, Texas. Ballengee has a passion for clarity of expectations. He has made his operating model explicit by creating an "expectations framework." This framework exists for everyone in the company and very clearly describes what is required to advance. It's not an evaluation or a commentary on what you've done but, rather, a road map for what you need to do to progress. Ballengee has documented his operating model, and the company reviews people's progress every three months.

As a consulting firm, Pariveda places great significance on its entrepreneurial employees doing things the Pariveda way. If you are a consultant at Pariveda, you'll have clear expectations in the following five categories:

- *Effectiveness*—Can you solve problems and work with people?

- *Business of information technology*—Is your knowledge increasing, and are you sharing your knowledge?

- *Others first*—Are you coaching, mentoring, and serving the community?

- *Relationships and sales*—Have you developed an account plan?

- *Leadership*—Do you have the key leadership attributes that will serve the company stakeholders, as well as contribute to your personal development?

By clarifying expectations and facilitating career growth, Pariveda delivers more value to its clients.

Five Entrepreneurial Beliefs

What's going on at Pierre and Pariveda? How does a food company break out of the grips of bankruptcy in the tightest credit market in fifty years? How does an IT consulting firm grow when most corporations are tightening their technology budgets?

The results described here are not happenstance. They result from a calculated effort to add clarity to expectations and to communicate a model for success. Bill Toler didn't model Pierre Foods after P&G and Nabisco. Instead, he took the best practices from the consumer packaging industry and the e-commerce market and built a business design and an operating model that made sense to his leadership team. Bruce Ballengee developed a model based on an expectations framework that was clear, concise, and communicable. Each of these leaders created components in the success of their business, and they are based on five entrepreneurial beliefs:

- Belief in the leader

- Belief in the purpose

- Belief in the operating model

- Belief in empowerment

- Belief in the reward

Let's look at these five beliefs in detail.

Belief in the Leader

When everyone in your organization believes in you as a leader, a high level of trust develops. Jim Kouzes and Barry Posner studied the characteristics of admired leaders in their book *The Leadership Challenge*. They found that the top characteristics of admired leaders were honesty, vision, and competence.[2] Belief in the leader means the people in your organization trust that you and the other leaders have integrity, competence, and vision. It means they believe you have the business acumen and talent to succeed, and they believe you are trustworthy.

Competence doesn't mean brilliance. In fact, Kouzes and Posner found that intelligence ranked low on their list of characteristics. You don't have to be the smartest person in your organization. Competence means you are reasonably smart (this is up to genetics) and you are constantly learning and growing (this is in your control). People want to know you try hard, make good decisions, and constantly learn. They want to know you are decisive.

What about trust? Humans don't instinctively trust each other. It's not in our genetic makeup. According to Watson Wyatt's annual workplace survey (WorkUS and WorkUK), only 50 percent of American workers have trust and confidence in the job being done by their organizations' leaders.[3]

We earn others' trust over time. To earn trust, leaders need to be trustworthy. Effective leaders engender trust by making and keeping commitments. They ensure their words and deeds are aligned with the best interest of the business. These same leaders know that when they make commitments to people and keep those commitments, they will be regarded as trustworthy. It's that simple.

If people realize the company's success takes precedence over the leaders' personal goals, they will trust the business. They want to know that you and the other leaders believe that your personal goals and objectives are best met when the business succeeds. Employees want to focus on building the business instead of worrying about hidden agendas. Furthermore, they want to stay focused on the customer instead of internal politics.

Nothing is worse than working for a manager who believes his own success is separate from the company's success. If you were an employee, where should your loyalties lie? Do you support the manager's agenda or the company's agenda? Even worse, you have to question whether your manager's behaviors are appropriate. He seems to be getting ahead by acting this way. Should you follow suit? The old adage that the best way to succeed is to find somebody already successful and copy his methods seems to apply. But does it?

If people in your organization are spending time answering these questions for themselves, they aren't spending time serving customers. You need to answer the questions for them. Make sure your entire leadership team puts the company's interests ahead of their own interests. When they do, trust will blossom in the organization.

Belief in the Purpose

Most people want to be a part of something big. They want to share in the creation of something important. And they want to believe in the purpose of their organization.

Leading companies have a strong purpose. For example, the stated purpose of Whole Foods Market is to allow common folks to buy the same high-quality products as rich people can. Microsoft's stated purpose is to enable people to have information at their fingertips. The Body Shop promotes social responsibility. Corporations with a clear purpose make it easier for employees to gain clarity on their personal business purpose. Employees know the business is trying to achieve something important and meaningful. They want more than a job. They want to be part of changing the world, even if it's just their own little corner of it.

To discover your company's purpose, ask yourself why your organization is important. If your company went out of business tomorrow or was reorganized out of existence, why would your customers care?

First consider your company's ideals and their importance. Why are ideals important? As Peter Marshall, chaplain of the U.S. Senate, said in 1947, "Give us clear vision, that we may know where to stand and what to stand for because unless we stand for something, we shall fall for anything."[4] This quote has been attributed to, among others, Alexander Hamilton and Ronald Reagan. But regardless of who said it, the point is that every business has to know what its ideals are. Why is it in business, and what is its real purpose for opening the doors every day?

When I was an executive with the Boeing Company, I attended Boeing's annual leadership summit in the very chic Century City section of Los Angeles. After opening the session with a fabulous Hollywood production showing all of Boeing's state-of-the-art hardware, Jim Albaugh, then president of the Boeing Integrated Defense Systems business unit, said, "Aren't you glad you don't make mayonnaise for a living?"

His question was meant not to slam the food industry. His point was that Boeing had a higher purpose everyone could get excited about.

So what is your company's purpose? Have you laid out a vision people can share? Are you constantly motivating everyone to make that vision a reality? What are your company's ideals?

The best ideals pass the test of time. They give meaning and relevance to your corporate activities and answer the question of why you open your doors every day, whether those doors are online or on Main Street. Ask yourself these questions when reviewing your ideals:

- What do you think about most often?

- Where do you spend most of your free time?

- Where do you spend your capital?

- What pleases you most about the direction of your business?

Once you have identified your organization's ideals, you can pass every tough question you'll ever face through your ideals filter. The answers to these tough questions may still be difficult to implement and even unpopular, but they will be aligned with your company values. And really, that is all your stakeholders want to see.

> **Once you have identified your organization's ideals, you can pass every tough question you'll ever face through your ideals filter.**

So now that you've aligned ideals with the purpose of your organization, you face no barriers to getting employees behind your stated purpose. When all employees in your organization share a belief in the purpose of the business, they stay focused on the big picture. Their actions become aligned with the direction of the business. Their collective thoughts center on better ways of achieving the purpose. They feel a sense of fulfillment that goes beyond just completing a task or job.

In order to believe in the purpose, they need to understand it. So you have to constantly repeat your stated purpose as if it were a mantra. It doesn't have to be earth shattering in its creativity or uniqueness; it just has to be yours.

How many times have you heard someone in your organization say, "We need a better understanding of where we are headed"? Too many managers are thrown off balance by that question. They can't understand why employees have a hard time understanding which direction the business is heading.

People need to know where they are going. They want to know that what they do every day contributes to the vision. To help them, many companies develop mission statements or vision statements. But a mission statement is only as good as the number of people who can live it every day. You need to put meaning behind the words of your mission statement.

To do this, identify the key words of your mission statement and then tell stories about people living those words. For example, if your mission statement says employees are going to be customer-focused, share company folklore that illustrates employees focusing on the customer. If your mission statement says employees are going to be a team, give examples of how teamwork helped win a new customer. Storytelling brings the words of your mission statement to life. Tell stories to customers, partners, and employees. Tell them to people you are trying to hire. Tell them to anyone who will listen.

Once employees understand the vision, they will live it. They will refine it based on their own experiences, and it will become the rallying cry of your organization. Your purpose will concentrate the creative energy of your people on helping your organization reach its goals.

Belief in the Operating Model

An operating model is the integration and interaction of your business constructs: the policies, procedures, processes, and structures of your business in dynamic interchange. It's *how* your business works. And your stakeholders need to believe in it.

Whether you know it or not, stakeholders (those who have an impact on your company or those on whom you have an impact) are constantly passing judgment on your operating model. They evaluate whether the model makes sense and compare it to other companies' models and to the models described in the business literature they read.

Every day, your employees pass judgment on your marketing strategy, accounting practices, management approach, hiring practices, and every other aspect of your business. They look for reasons to believe your operating model makes sense. Your job is to help them find those reasons.

When employees believe in your operating model, they understand it. They understand the rationale behind the processes, policies, and procedures you have implemented. Equipped to make decisions, they frame every decision in the purpose of the company and an understanding of business financials.

Your job as a leader is to share the operating model with all your employees so they can demonstrate their knowledge and align their daily activities with the purpose of the business. The people in your organization have to know that you take the operating model very seriously. You must show them that the operating model was designed to help the business achieve its purpose. Talk to them about it at every opportunity. Your operating model has to be a reflection of what you believe and what you want for your business.

The operating model is that important. Why? Because it's not *what* you do; it's *how* you do it.

You probably aren't offering a product or service that is completely unique. Most likely, you have some competition. To be different, you have to develop an operating model that reflects your unique vision of what your customers need. And you have to ensure everyone believes it will succeed.

Belief in Empowerment

The real benefit of working in an Internal Franchise is that people can act on their own with the full support and backing of the organization. In an Internal Franchise, all employees act like stewards or owners of the business. Therefore, you authorize them to make decisions, and even more significant, you train them to make the *right* decisions. Authorizing people to make decisions is not enough. They won't act unless they feel confident they can act appropriately.

When employees believe in empowerment, they believe in the organization and in themselves. They know the organization supports their actions, and they will likely make the right decisions. Most importantly, they know they are allowed to fail. Mistakes are tolerated because your people learn from mistakes and avoid repeating them.

For example, a good friend of mine once made the mistake of the century. He signed a $1 million fixed-price contract without checking a box that requested progress payments. In other words, he signed a contract that required the company to deliver $1 million worth of services without receiving any form of payment until the entire job was complete, almost nine months later. In essence, he created a massive cash-flow problem for the company.

His first response (after the tears stopped) was to control the damage. The company set out to control expenses and raise cash until payment was received. Once the immediate cash-flow crisis was solved, my friend met with the company's legal staff to ensure that a process was put into place so that the problem would never occur again. He shared the story with everyone (even though he took a lot of ribbing) so no one would make the same mistake. In the end, the company survived, and everyone learned from the experience. More importantly, everyone realized the company could tolerate mistakes as long as the people involved learned a constructive lesson and took action to avoid repeating the mistake.

People believe in empowerment when they have the authority to act, the ability to act, and support when they do act. When they believe in it, they feel a sense of purpose and fulfillment that goes beyond financial compensation. Employees today want to feel empowered, and they want opportunity. They want to grow and have an impact on the organization.

> **People believe in empowerment when they have the authority to act, the ability to act, and support when they do act.**

Belief in the Reward

How many of us would continue at our jobs if we didn't get paid? Unfortunately, not many of us are that fond of our jobs. Let's face it: the reward is a major reason for doing what we do, but reward includes much more than just money.

When employees believe in the reward, they believe that when the business succeeds, they will succeed. They are willing to give their best efforts on behalf of the business because they know their personal success is tied to the success of the business. This is constantly on their minds. Help your people stay focused on the big picture. In turn, they will try to improve the business so that their reward increases. Employees will think and act like entrepreneurs, like owners of the business. They'll protect the bottom line as if it's their own because it is their own!

Remember that people act as they are measured. If you measure and tie bonuses to key management indicators that do not build long-term business value, you're in trouble. But if you start with behaviors you desire, such as making raving fans out of your clients or building a workplace culture that attracts and retains the best personnel, you can find ways to measure elements of the behaviors that will lead to the business results you desire.

Further evidence of creating a belief in the reward comes from Malcolm Gladwell. Gladwell's book *Outliers: The Story of Success* contains a fascinating story about the work habits of the typical Asian rice farmer. In a nutshell, Gladwell suggests that work can be rewarding to the individual and beneficial to the organization (or society) if it follows these principles:

- *Meaningful*—The connection between effort and reward is clear.

- *Complex*—The problem set is sufficiently challenging.

- *Autonomous*—One can make and implement decisions on one's own.[5]

Any leader attempting to build reward systems while ignoring these simple principles does so at her own peril. Let's discuss these in a little more detail.

- *Meaningful*—Work that is meaningful reflects who we are and not just what we do. Make sure your team understands that the extraordinary effort you are asking for will be fairly, and perhaps handsomely, rewarded. Don't scrimp on the reward. Make it clear, straightforward, and as close as possible to real-time.

- *Complex*—Mundane work numbs the brain. Innovation suffers in an environment where the rules are overbearing. Old market rules that once applied will be followed until either the market dries up or you are run out by the competition. Complexity can be the secret sauce that challenges the workforce to stay relevant in their skills and abilities. Always encourage your team to be creative in their approach to your business challenges.

- *Autonomous*—Individuals or teams that get to decide for themselves how the work should be performed are typically closer aligned to the realities of the business. Teach your team the rules of your business, and allow them to surprise you.

Without a belief in the reward, people lose their entrepreneurial drive and begin to wonder why they are working so hard. If employees begin to lose the sense of purpose, fulfillment, and opportunity that has been fueling their ambition, it is only natural for them to begin to look for new opportunities that may better fulfill their desire for reward. As a leader, you'll begin to notice a less-productive and less-focused workforce when employees lose interest in the business while salaries and bonuses become entitlements. Even your most dependable employee will lose the sense of connection between pay and performance. The rewards your employees anticipate for the work they do is directly proportional to the level of trust they have in the leader or institution.

The Power of Trust

Imagine that you didn't have complete belief and trust in your bank (not really a stretch these days). Imagine that you weren't 100 percent convinced your money would be there when you went to get it. How paralyzing that would be! You would be afraid to deposit a paycheck. You would probably check your available balance several times each day. Your attention during the day would dwell on your bank and not on the more important aspects in life. In the end, you would take your money somewhere else, even if it meant putting it under your mattress.

The ability to trust and believe in a system is the key determinant of the system's success—even if the system is a business. If employees don't believe in the operating model, they cannot be effective. This lack of belief manifests itself in many ways, including these:

- Employees watch their backs instead of focusing on the customer.

- They spend time looking for hidden agendas.

- They work to beat internal systems rather than improve them.

- They engage in petty politics. When this happens, trust becomes nonexistent. In the end, good employees will take their services somewhere else.

- Trusting the system is liberating. It frees up an enormous amount of time to focus on more important things. In this case, employees focus on the customer. And the employees are free to place their trust in their leaders.

Conclusion

When employees believe in the leaders, they adopt the leaders' beliefs and values. When they believe in the purpose of a business, they become prophets and spread its message to anyone who will listen. When they believe in empowerment, they act. And when they understand the operating model, they act appropriately. When they believe that they will succeed when the business succeeds, they'll focus their attention on the success of the business, nothing else.

When the five entrepreneurial beliefs are inculcated in your culture, your business will become a finely tuned system and your people will become a team. They'll believe in the game plan and focus on winning. The business will begin to operate on its own, without your constant attention. You will have more time to work on the business instead of working in the business. With more time, you can improve the company's operating model, find new opportunities, develop more people, and stay focused on the changing market.

Make certain all the people in your organization believe in the leadership of your company. Confirm that they believe in the purpose of your business. Ensure that they believe in the operating model and that they believe in empowerment and the reward. Then, let them go. Get out of their way. Release the power of your people. Discover how powerful a company of entrepreneurs can be. Discover the power of an Internal Franchise to transform your organization into a raging success!

2

Branding Your Workplace

"CULTURE" IS ONE of the strongest words in our lexicon. *Webster's New International Dictionary* defines it as "an integrated pattern of human behavior that includes thought, speech, actions and artifacts."[1] Culture embodies the shared principles and values that bind people together and define the boundaries of acceptable behavior. These boundaries determine which behaviors we reward and which behaviors we punish. When individuals encounter such boundaries, they make a conscious decision to live within them or to cross over them. Their decisions have real and important consequences, including the loss of life or liberty.

Cultures can have a natural beauty, as well as a dark and ugly side. A culture can be the foundation of a lasting civilization, or it can promote a xenophobic attitude leading to forms of sectarian violence. With the majesty of a country's culture come elements of nationalism, which, if channeled incorrectly, can lead an entire nation down a path of destruction. Yet we all desire to be part of a strong culture in our daily lives. We teach our children about our culture. We fight to keep it stable and consistent, and we want to be part of it at home and at work.

Corporate Culture

In much the same way, a corporate culture includes the shared principles and values that bind together the people in an organization. It operates unconsciously beneath the surface, controlling the behavior of everyone who works in the organization.

A corporate culture defines how everyone in an organization acts and behaves. It dictates what behavior is accepted and what is frowned upon. It sets the stage for what an organization tries to achieve. Corporate culture is born from principles and values but is nurtured and shaped by specific actions and reward systems. It's solidified when an organization experiences success or failure. So how does your business get a corporate culture?

Mission statements and corporate creeds sometimes document and codify corporate cultures. In other cases, a corporate culture embodies a set of unwritten rules that propagate throughout the organization because of the words and deeds of the organization's leaders. It lives in all businesses, whether acknowledged explicitly or not. It may not be a productive culture, and it may not be a desired culture. It may be a positive force, or it may be a destructive force. It may contribute to growth, or it may be a drag on the business. But it's a culture nonetheless, and it's constantly at work influencing the actions of the people in the organization. The challenge is to observe it, define it, and leverage its power to affect your organization's success.

This chapter describes what a corporate culture is, how to identify it, and why it's important. Then, it explains culture's role in aligning your people with your business goals. We'll also explore an "ownership culture"—the binding agent in an Internal

Franchise—and its role as the corporate culture of choice. We'll look at the principles and values of an ownership culture as the franchise agreement in your Internal Franchise. Finally, we'll illustrate how an ownership culture can help brand your workplace and help you attract, motivate, and retain the people you need.

You Know It When You See It

When you think about corporate culture, you might conjure up images of an IBM salesperson from the 1970s, dressed in a white shirt and a dark suit. Or you may think about young, smart, aggressive engineers, dressed in shorts and sandals, working around the clock for a Silicon Valley start-up during the dot-com days. Perhaps the carefree and humorous culture of Outback Steakhouse or the formal, buttoned-down culture of a Wall Street law firm comes to mind. A corporate culture is difficult to define, but to paraphrase Justice Potter Stewart, "you know it when you see it."[2]

Often, the most visible parts of a corporate culture are the sets of expected behaviors the organization tends to enforce. You can see it at work when new employees join a team. Immediately, certain behaviors are encouraged or rejected. Aggressive behavior might be rejected, or consensus building might be encouraged. Whatever the case, new employees adhere to the unwritten rules about expected behavior or they don't fit in.

Most of the time corporate cultures just seem to evolve without any conscious effort. In many organizations, a key leader's particular style, personality, or belief system is the genesis of the culture. Other cultures are formed like glaciers, shaped by the thawing and refreezing of corporate initiatives and influenced by the external conditions of the marketplace. Whatever its starting point, the culture propagates across the organization through conversations with employees and through actions that are consistent with the core principles and values of the culture.

In *Leadership Jazz*, Max De Pree discusses the role of water-carriers in spreading the culture in early Native American tribes.[3] The watercarrier—the tribal storyteller—shared stories that connected people and tribes. In companies, leaders play this role, reinforcing the culture in every word they speak and action they take. By virtue of their position, leaders are watercarriers; they are the company storytellers. They convey accepted behaviors, teach the operating model of the company, and strengthen, for good or bad, the bonds that link the people to each other and the organization. Employees observe the leaders and draw conclusions about what is important and acceptable. Over time, what is important to the leaders takes root in the culture of the company. The culture is cemented, either positively or negatively, when the organization experiences success or failure. Here are a few examples of corporate culture.

"It's Only Rock 'n' Roll"

Barrie Bergman is a veteran empire builder who never played by the rules. Bergman was the CEO of the Record Bar, a record store with 180 locations in thirty states, and Bare Escentuals, a 24-store mineral makeup company. Bergman's key to success was never taking himself too seriously. He'd say, "It's only rock 'n' roll." Bergman built workplace cultures based on integrity and trust, with philosophies such as "Treat people like they are honest, and they'll reward you with honesty." Bergman lived by the golden rule, and he expected others to do the same.

While at the Record Bar, he created a "my store mentality." In this culture, managers' compensation was tied to their performance. The Record Bar promoted from within, so store clerks could see themselves becoming store managers. The culture rejected meetings as a form of management and required all managers to continue pushing decisions down to the lowest level.

Did it work? Bergman and his team built great value in the Record Bar and sold it for $92 million. Fourteen years after acquiring the fledgling four-store Bare Escentuals, they recapitalized that company for $200 million.[4]

Culture matters!

"This Integrity Stuff Is New to Us"

For many years, my wife worked in the consumer packaged goods industry. She tells this story, and it has become one of my favorite corporate culture examples.

The protagonist in this drama is a wholesale food company. We'll call it Diversion Distributors to protect the innocent (or should we say the guilty?). Consumer products manufacturers have historically had a big problem called product diversion. Product diversion occurs when a manufacturer produces a product and ships it to a wholesaler, and then, the wholesaler diverts the product into another market. The wholesaler makes a profit by buying the product at a discount in New England, for example, and then shipping it to another part of the country where the manufacturer hasn't discounted the price. Diversion Distributors did this for years and was repeatedly warned about the unethical nature of this practice by the manufacturer.

Finally, the manufacturer decided to put the squeeze on Diversion. Its executives threatened to stop using Diversion's distribution facilities if the practice didn't stop. They lectured Diversion on integrity and character and how this practice hurt the manufacturer's business in other parts of the country. Two warnings later, Diversion still had not changed its ways, so the manufacturer terminated the relationship. The companies would no longer do business together.

Diversion was shocked. This manufacturer represented 30 percent of its business base, and it would have a difficult time surviving if it lost this piece of its business. The president of Diversion literally chased the manufacturer's executives into the parking lot, pleading for one more chance. Diversion had been conducting this unethical practice for so long, it simply was part of the culture. The executives of the manufacturing firm fired back with a lecture on the importance of building partnerships, maintaining relationships, and working as a team. Finally, the president of Diversion dropped his head and said, "Look, we're trying. Give us another chance. This integrity stuff is new to us."

Treasure Quest

Sometimes the culture is defined by the market. Consider Odyssey Marine Exploration, based in Tampa, Florida. Odyssey is the world leader in deep-ocean shipwreck exploration, searching the globe's vast oceans for sunken ships with intriguing stories, extraordinary treasure, and precious artifacts spanning centuries of maritime travel. If you are a fan of the Discovery Channel, you may be familiar with Odyssey through the series *Treasure Quest*.

Virtually every employee at Odyssey works there because of what the company does. CEO Mark Gordon calls it "living a childhood dream."[5] The mission of the company is compelling, but Odyssey's leaders are not content with letting the treasure-hunter moniker be the company's only cultural attribute. Although Odyssey is a publicly traded company, it still makes time for events like town hall meetings, mini-parties to celebrate birthdays, and Oktoberfest. Many times, the small actions that leaders take are what characterize the culture and make employees want to go the extra mile for the company.

Odyssey also makes it very clear to the staff that treasure hunting is a capital-intense operation and balancing risk with outcomes is critical for its long-term corporate health. Odyssey has decided that the company's mission can attract the kind of people it is looking for, but to turn those thrill-seeking employees into treasure-hunting professionals who understand how the company makes money takes the right blend of cultural norms and business practices. Culture matters.

Why Corporate Culture Is Important

Have you ever driven a car in need of a front-end alignment? As you drive down the road, you can feel that the car has a natural drift in one direction or another. Take your hands off the steering wheel for even a second, and the car automatically begins to drift. On a long trip, the fight to keep the car going in the correct direction wears you out. Over time, the bad alignment will cause undue wear and tear on the tires and the suspension system and result in expensive repairs.

The same drift occurs in a business without a corporate culture that supports and enhances its business vision. It's out of alignment. It takes a tremendous amount of the leadership's time and energy to constantly monitor the direction the organization is heading and to bring it back into alignment when necessary. Over time, if the misalignment isn't fixed, extensive damage can occur—especially in a competitive, rapidly changing business environment.

When Paul Silber was the CEO of the Baltimore-based In Vitro Technologies, a contract research company that sold for a premium valuation in 2006, he was always looking for ways to make In Vitro more efficient or lean. Silber found that what had started out as the "ten commandments" of how things should work had morphed into "five hundred commandments" as the company grew. All the changes were well-intentioned but productivity was really starting to slow down because "how things should work" was not the same as "how things actually worked." In Vitro's leaders thus had to redirect their attention to the reality of how work got done in order to meet their demanding performance objectives. The cultural attribute of efficiency had been beaten over the head by the cultural attribute of process formalization. Getting lean and reinforcing the cultural attributes that went along with the ten commandments would be key for In Vitro's success.

This is a classic example of misalignment in a business. The leadership of this business created an operating model that worked so well, it had the potential to serve as many customers as time would allow. Yet, the company drifted away from its early cultural norms.

You may be experiencing something like this in your organization. Shifting accepted behavior here and dropping your guard there eventually leads to a tipping point. Over time, the company becomes something you no longer recognize. And without governance and insight, the leadership might not even know it—just like the slow damage caused by a bad front-end alignment.

In the current business environment, a great product or service no longer suffices. Success or failure is determined by how well an organization can align, inspire, and mobilize people around its strategy. The efficient use of capital and equipment, long the hallmark of good management, must now incorporate the best use of human resources. In other words, business success today is directly proportionate to the number of people within your company who truly understand how the business works and who are motivated to make the business a success. That's why your culture is so important. It keeps your entire organization aligned with your business goals.

Three Kinds of Culture

In *Corporate Culture and Performance*, John Kotter and James Heskett explored the link between corporate culture and business performance. They identified three types of cultures: a strong culture, a strategically appropriate culture, and an adaptive culture.[6]

Strong Culture

A strong culture is easy to identify. Everyone in the organization shares a consistent set of values and methods of doing business. Accounting firms, law firms, and many federal government agencies are good examples of strong cultures. In organizations with strong cultures, everyone seems alike. From the outside, the organization seems to have a style or a way of working. On the inside, there is a feeling of homogeneity.

I experienced a strong culture at a meeting with one of the largest law firms in Dallas. When I arrived at the firm and began preparing for the meeting, I could feel the strong culture as it surrounded us in mahogany and leather. The players at this meeting were all high-priced litigators. Although each attorney was very successful in his own right, all of them had the same uniform: suspenders, Mont Blanc pens, more starched shirts, and cufflinks—lots of cufflinks. As this group of lawyers shifted positions and moved their arms as they sat around that mahogany table, those cufflinks created a percussion section that would make the New York Philharmonic proud. Strong cultures typically have very visible outward signs like this.

So is a strong culture good? Is it something for which you want to strive? One of the weaknesses of companies that have strong cultures is their inability to adapt. Companies with strong cultures often stumble because their norms and behaviors have been shaped over years of success, and it becomes very difficult to change and innovate. "This is the way we do things" is a typical mantra in a strong culture. When the competitive environment changes, these companies discover they are out of sync. They lose ground to companies that have the second type of culture: a strategically appropriate culture.

Strategically Appropriate Culture

A strategically appropriate culture is one that fits the current industry or business climate. For example, if the business climate demands quality products and customer service, those companies with cultures that encourage quality and customer service perform better.

Over the short term, organizations with strategically appropriate cultures have an advantage over companies with strong cultures because their mode of operations just happens to match what the market is demanding. But Kotter and Heskett discovered that a strategically appropriate culture wasn't enough to guarantee long-term success either. They found the companies that performed best over a long period of time had adaptive cultures.[7]

Adaptive Culture

An adaptive culture is a way of operating where changes are expected and adapting to those changes is routine and seamless. Adaptive cultures can rapidly adapt to meet new market demands because change, growth, and innovation are a given part of the business environment.

Apple's culture is a good example of an adaptive culture. When the entertainment industry was shifting to file sharing and MP3 players, Apple was able to adapt and discovered a brilliant way to leverage its skills, competencies, and understanding of the culture. This adaptation was not just the introduction of a new product (the iPod); it was a fundamental change in the way the company looked at the market. No longer was it going to be a bit player in the PC market; it was going to adapt and dominate the portable music player market. Apple's culture promotes flexibility and competitive drive.

An adaptive culture is what businesses should want. The last five years of shifting consumer demand have seen the market swallow many companies. Some of the companies that have weathered the worst economic conditions in fifty years have been able to survive because of their ability to adapt. They've been able to react quickly to market conditions, leverage their competencies in new markets, and modify their products and services to meet the current demands of consumers. Those companies that could not adapt have been forced to undergo painful downsizing and reengineering. The ability to change and adapt is a critical success factor in business today.

The Adaptive Culture of Choice

The word "change" is overused today, but change is a fact of business life. However, it doesn't just create problems. It creates opportunities for companies to harness change for business growth. Those companies charging into these uncharted waters aren't being hampered by change but are instead exploiting it. They're looking for business opportunities at the intersection of changing human needs and innovation. This helps them ensure their business design delivers value to the customer while generating a profit for the company. Furthermore, they're building operating models and developing cultures that breed innovation and a genuine interest in the customer.

Corporate culture is the most important tool a company possesses to help capitalize on the constant and accelerating pace of change. But not just any culture will work. It must be an ownership culture!

An ownership culture is the ultimate adaptive culture because everyone in the organization acts like an owner of the business. Every business owner knows the importance of being flexible. Saying no to a customer request is forbidden. You find a way to meet the request, no matter what. The focus is on the customer and on making the business a success. When everyone acts like an owner, employees feel empowered and in control. In this culture, an organization can thrive in an environment of rapid change.

Your culture defines how people in your organization act. When you implement an Internal Franchise, employees act like business owners. They stay focused on the customer yet are flexible and adapt to new competitive challenges. Employees understand every aspect of the business and can identify areas of improvement. This leads them to work *on* the business instead of just working *in* the business. They don't just manage; they lead. They believe in the business and trust that when the business succeeds, so will they.

And when you create an ownership culture based on the five entrepreneurial beliefs discussed in chapter 1—belief in the leader, the purpose, the operating model, empowerment, and the reward—you will motivate these behaviors. This will establish the values of the entrepreneur as the foundation of your culture. Let's look at these values in detail.

Entrepreneurial Values

The first value is *customers*. In an ownership culture, everyone in the organization values customers and watches for changes in customers' needs and demands. Everyone knows who the ultimate customers are and routinely looks for the best new ways to serve them. I can't imagine a company doing a better job at this than King Arthur Flour. To give you a little perspective, King Arthur has been listening to its customers since George Washington was president! It is America's oldest flour company, and it decided years ago that an educated consumer was going to be a loyal and dedicated consumer. King Arthur Flour built the Baking Education Center in Norwich, Vermont, as a way to promote baking and educate consumers on the need for pure, high-quality, and consistently performing flour, which just happens to be what King Arthur Flour makes.

Flexibility, the second value, is essential when serving customers. A company with an ownership culture quickly develops ways to adapt to new customer priorities and market trends. It is simply unacceptable to miss an opportunity because of arduous administrative analysis or bungling bureaucratic backbiting. Everyone understands that the most potent competitor may not be the behemoth down the street. It's more likely to be the aggressive start-up whose teeth have been sharpened by survival techniques.

People working in an ownership culture also stay focused on the *big picture*, the third value. In an ownership culture, it's not the responsibility of a few executives to recite the corporate mission. The mission is part of the way the entire company performs its daily activities. All the decision makers in the organization understand that the decisions they make in their own area of responsibility will have an impact on other parts of the company. They understand how a narrow focus can hurt the company. Here's one example.

Whole Foods Market has become a very large corporation, but one of the keys to continued success has been the role of the store manager or store team leaders. In essence, each store team leader is running an Internal Franchise of Whole Foods. Each store team leader has great autonomy and always balances the needs of the customers with the desires of the bean counter, sitting at headquarters in Austin, Texas.

During an interview with Mark Ehrnstein, Whole Foods' global vice president of team member services, I mentioned that during the Mid-Atlantic Blizzard of February 2010, we were able to buy staples from the Annapolis, Maryland, store well after normal closing time. In fact, it was close to 11:00 p.m. Mark indicated he was aware of this and explained that the store team leader had made the decision to keep the store open because it was in the best interest of the community. Mark also shared the story of a store team leader in New York who gave away perishable products for three hours during a power outage. You may argue that the product would have spoiled anyway, but few other grocery stores would make such a business decision.

Executives and managers need to understand the current condition in the market to make sure they are meeting the needs of their customers while still meeting the obligations of their stakeholders. On the other hand, they also need to be fully aware that one parochial decision or statement made in haste can have a dramatic effect on the organization.

An ownership culture also embraces *leadership*, the fourth entrepreneurial value. Leaders in ownership cultures focus on developing a workforce that is empowered and has significant input into the direction and success of the organization. These leaders find a way to breed and nurture a company of employees focused on serving their customers and eager to see the company succeed. They find a way to motivate skeptical employees who question the purpose of the company.

A productive workforce won't wait for the leaders to make the rules, choose the teams, and blow the whistle. Employees want and deserve to be part of the rule making and breaking. They will be the ones who establish the principles and values and reinforce the culture. Leaders in an ownership culture embrace this approach and capitalize on it for the benefit of the entire organization.

Culture as a Brand

A company's ability to attract, motivate, and retain its highly skilled workers is critical to its continued success. Many companies use and replace employees at such high rates that it affects their growth and profitability. Worse, some companies compete for new workers solely on the basis of the financial bottom line. Higher salaries, more benefits, and higher bonus payments are just some of the ways companies increase their hiring costs. Unfortunately, someone else is always willing to pay a little more. So, the price of hiring employees continues to rise even while turnover increases.

Competing on price never works. You can't build customer loyalty on low prices alone, and you can't build employee loyalty by just paying higher salaries. You have a choice: you can position your company, or you can compete. Positioning means value, image, and leadership. Competing means price wars, higher costs, more turnover, and dissatisfied customers.

To help your company attract, motivate, and retain the people you need, you must position the workplace environment as a truly remarkable and unique place to work. You accomplish this by branding your workplace.

In times of rampant change, brands are a powerful source of continuity and trust. The fundamental purpose of brands is to create stakeholder loyalty and preference over the long term. Brands are a little bit like a child's blanket in that they provide a level of comfort and a degree of security in times of economic instability. When economic conditions improve and companies begin to forecast a certain level of prosperity, brands offer opportunity.

When we think of brands, we normally think of the products and companies in *BusinessWeek*'s annual review of brands. According to *BusinessWeek*, the top 10 Global Brands for 2009 were Coca-Cola, IBM, Microsoft, GE, Nokia, McDonald's, Google, Toyota, Intel, and Disney.[8] It is probably no surprise to us that ubiquitous Google was the fastest growing brand in 2009. Brands are an ever-present part of our lives. From the clothes we wear to the food we eat, from the toys our children play with to the drinks we consume, from our mobile phones and search engines to our expensive cars, brands are everywhere.

The most successful brands are ones that build trust. They cultivate an image, persona, or personality that appeals to a specific target audience and gives them comfort that they are making the right decision. When I first entered the workforce, a saying in the tech sector was that IT executives would never be fired for buying IBM products. CIOs' offices felt a sense of security with the IBM brand. Even my children value a sense of brand security. If given the choice between an iPod or some other MP3 players, they want the Apple product. They just trust the name!

But why are brands so powerful? First, they nurture increased customer loyalty. Consumers develop a strong affiliation with particular brands. Therefore, they feel a commitment or even an obligation to purchase or use a particular brand. In the same way, employees will develop a strong affiliation with your company and your culture. The employee retention rate goes up because employees and prospective employees trust that this is the place to continue their careers. Not only does a strong workplace brand help in recruiting and retention, it has a practical element in that it saves your company thousands of dollars in hiring and training costs.

Second, brands differentiate. In competitive markets, brands offer a means of differentiating products and services that in many ways are identical. So, a strong workplace brand helps you differentiate your company. Although the unemployment rate is higher than it's been in a quarter century and many markets have very little competition for employees, that situation will certainly change. As markets and sectors expand, companies with trusted workplace brands will attract the best people.

A number of years ago I joined an IT services company named Conquest as its COO. After working there for a few months and being very impressed with the talent level, I had a meeting with Lee Walker, the CEO of Innovative Engineering Solutions, which was one of our competitors. Lee asked me how I liked my new role at Conquest. Then he said, "You know, they have all the good people." One of the reasons Conquest attracted "all the good people" was because it had successfully turned its workplace culture into a brand that had tangible value. A company must stand out as a truly remarkable place to work in order to attract the people it needs. Your company must become a *destination* for prospective employees.

Third, brands allow better pricing. Because of the assurance of quality often associated with a brand, the manufacturer can often charge a premium price. Don't you think Apple is turning a substantial profit on every $500 iPad sold? Even more important, strong brands can often undercut rivals without creating a low-quality image, simply because their names are better known or associated with certain characteristics, such as quality, style, or even sex appeal. Likewise, a strong workplace brand helps you break out of the cycle of price competition regarding salaries. For example, Odyssey Marine Exploration pays fair salaries, but it doesn't have to overpay for top talent because it leverages its "treasure hunters" workplace brand.

Prospective employees are attracted to your company not solely because of salary and perks but also because of the intangibles of working in your culture. Here are three factors that you should consider to realize the benefits of a workplace brand in your organization.

Credibility

Your claims about your workplace environment must be built on a solid foundation of truth. A claim without substance won't work. It's not enough to say that your company is a truly unique place to work; it must *be* a truly unique place to work.

Every year, *Fortune* magazine publishes a list of the greatest places to work. One of the best companies for all thirteen years of the list has been SAS. SAS is the leader in *business analytics* software and services and is the largest independent vendor in the business intelligence market. It also boasts a laundry list of benefits: high-quality childcare at $410 a month, 90 percent coverage of the health insurance premium, unlimited sick days, a medical center staffed by four physicians and ten nurse practitioners (at no cost to employees), a free 66,000-square-foot fitness center and indoor swimming pool, a lending library, and a summer camp for children. It has a culture, according to Jim Goodnight, the company's cofounder and the only CEO that SAS has had in its thirty-four-year history, based on "trust between our employees and the company."[9]

A number of regional publications also publish lists of great places to work. *Baltimore Magazine* recognized CollabraSpace, a privately held provider of Web-based collaboration solutions.[10] CollabraSpace provides 100 percent employer-paid health insurance and a four-week paid sabbatical after five years of service. Employees also like the equity awards for all employees if the company meets its goals, bonus plans, and profit sharing.

Other great places to work include Edward Jones, Wegmans, Google, Boston Consulting Group, and Qualcomm. They all have strong workplace brands.

To see if your company has a credible brand, identify three to five unique truths about the workplace environment that you can easily prove to prospective employees. For example, do you empower workers? Prove it. Do you respect your workers? Share company stories that show how. Do you offer increased authority and responsibility? Let prospective employees talk to your current employees to verify your claim. Your claims must be based on truth. Everyone in the organization must believe that these truths exist and

> **To see if your company has a credible brand, identify three to five unique truths about the workplace environment that you can easily prove to prospective employees.**

will continue to exist. And credibility starts at the top of the organization—with you!

Customization

Your workplace brand must be customized to your target audience. Think about what type of employees you seek to attract. Does your hiring process focus on filling technical slots, or are you more interested in attracting employees who have the ability and desire to add value to the organization? One senior executive of a consumer packaging company complained that he had difficulty attracting the very best technical talent to his organization. He had his pick of top-sales professionals, but he never seemed to attract great technical staff for his information systems department. Talented technology employees simply did not view this particular company as an attractive alternative because it wasn't thought of as a leading-edge technology company.

If you want employees who will act like owners of your business, your culture must attract these people. You must be able to express how the workplace environment addresses the needs of this type of employee. We'll discuss entrepreneurial talent in great detail in chapter 4, but your ability to match the specific attributes of your culture to the needs and expectations of employees is the essence of building a workplace brand.

Independence

Your workplace environment must be able to stand on its own, separate from the leaders of your organization and separate from the specific products and services your organization provides. As an example, ad agencies often try to attract talented creative designers by offering them the opportunity to build a world-class portfolio. This is the wrong approach. The agencies are not building equity in their workplace environment. They are building equity in what the employees do.

As another example, an executive of a technology consulting firm found that he was able to hire people because they were excited about working for a particular customer it had. It seems this customer had the latest technology that most technicians covet. However, if the company loses that customer, where do you think those employees will go? Once again, the owner of this company is not building equity in his workplace brand.

For your workplace brand to be independent, people must rate the environment or culture as a major factor in why they came to work for your company. King Arthur Flour's culture can stand on its own, and one of the reasons is its inclusiveness. The company communicates just about everything to all the people in the organization, which, in turn, empowers them as partners in the endeavor. One of the reasons for the high retention of employees at King Arthur Flour is that people are attracted to this inclusiveness and can't find it in other workplaces.

When your workplace environment is credible, customized, and independent, you have created a workplace brand that has legs and can be leveraged for business success.

Conclusion

An ownership culture is part of an organization's brand identity. It defines the value proposition offered to employees. Therefore, having an ownership culture is a powerful way to build employee loyalty and motivation at a time when attracting, motivating, and retaining people are critical to your success.

An ownership culture is also the agreement in your Internal Franchise. Although it may not be a legal document, it's just as binding. It establishes the principles that govern everyone's activities within the organization. It provides boundaries for acceptable behavior, including exercising initiative, accepting accountability, working as a team, and staying focused on the customer. It elevates the ideal that what's good for the business is good for *everyone* in the business. It embraces the values of the entrepreneur. It motivates everyone to think and act like an owner when executing the company's operating model.

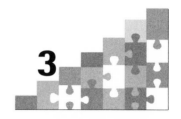

3

Modeling
Your Business

A MODEL IS a miniature representation of a working system. It depicts selected characteristics of the system for which it stands. It's useful to the extent that it accurately portrays those characteristics that happen to be of interest at the moment. Models can change over time based on environmental or market conditions. For example, the model of the Deepwater Horizon oil platform before the spill was certainly not the same as the model after the spill.

Let's take a moment to look at the kinds of systems we have in business. Systems in the business world can be characterized as simple, complicated, and complex. Simple systems are time-tested procedures; complicated systems require the procedures, as well as additional expertise; complex systems add a dimension of unpredictability to even the most complicated systems.

In simple systems, like baking a pie, a recipe is essential. It's tested by generations of bakers to ensure easy replication without the need for any particular expertise. Recipes produce standardized products, and the best recipes give good results every time. The same can be said for most business process procedures. If a procedure is well documented, it can be performed by someone with less expertise than the creator of the procedure.

Complicated systems, like building custom Web applications in the software world or sending a shuttle into space, are different. Formulas or recipes are critical and necessary to solve the problems associated with these systems, but they are often not sufficient. High levels of expertise in a variety of fields are required. For example, a scientist's launching of one rocket helps ensure that the next mission will be a success. In some critical ways, rockets are similar to each other; therefore, a relatively high degree of certainty of the outcome exists.

Raising children, on the other hand, is a complex system. A recipe or formula has a much more limited application. Ask any parent: raising one child provides experience but certainly does not ensure success with the next. Although expertise can contribute to the process in valuable ways, it provides neither necessary nor sufficient conditions to ensure success. Every child is unique and must be parented as an individual. As a result, some uncertainty of the outcome always exists. However, the complexity of the process and the lack of certainty don't lead us to the conclusion that it's impossible to raise a child.

In an Internal Franchise, we have an operating model, engaged entrepreneurial employees, and a culture of ownership. As you begin to create the operating model of your business, consider the parts of your business that are simple, complicated, and complex. When modeling your enterprise, make every attempt to simplify the business. Operating models should be readily understood. However, that does not mean you need to dumb down the business. Most businesses have components that are complicated and some even have complex systems, but this fact should not stop you from modeling the business in a way that can be easily communicated and replicated.

Here is a quick test to see if you are able to communicate your operating model. If you can explain to your teenager what you do and she understands, you're on the right track. If she has a perplexed look after you explain what you do for a living, you've got some work to do.

The discipline of modeling will help you accurately depict those characteristics that are important when you devise an operating model to internally franchise to your employees. The purpose of specifying your operating model is to build consensus on the key elements of your business and to teach everyone in your organization about the business. Therefore, the model you build must help you achieve these objectives.

The business model consists of the following elements:

- Business focus

- Financial model

- Operating parameters

- Core processes

These four areas encapsulate the critical aspects of any business: customers, finances, operations, and processes. If you can accurately depict these elements, you can develop an effective model of your entire business—an operating model. Then, you can ensure everyone in your organization is working toward a common goal.

The business focus starts with what you do and for whom you do it. This focus defines who your customers are and what you offer them. It also defines the promise you make to customers every time they make a purchase. And you want everyone in your organization to understand that!

The financial model determines how your business makes money or, in the case of not-for-profits, clarifies the role finances play in daily operations. Everyone in the company contributes to the profitability of the business, and the financial model operationalizes the details of the financial statements.

Operationalizing the vision defines the operating reality of your business. Done right, it will depict what your business vision really means operationally. Operational effectiveness is essential for any business, but it is certainly not sufficient for long-term success. Well-defined operating parameters help your employees align their contribution to the daily success of the business and give those employees an opportunity to live the company vision every day.

Core processes are the foundation for any business that has graduated from the incubator stage. They clarify what needs to happen every day and are the engine that drives business success. To be effective, all the people in the organization must understand how the business works, and they must constantly strive to improve its ability to deliver value to your customers.

When everyone in your company intuitively understands what you do and for whom you do it, contributes to your business's profitability, and executes its core processes like an expert, you have a recipe for business success.

Let's look at these essential elements of your business in more detail.

Business Focus

A business's natural tendency is to try to be all things to all people. In an ad on my local radio station, a company states, "No customer is too small or too large!" Another company does "major and minor construction projects!" Can you really have it both ways? Is your target market everyone? Do you offer anything to anyone with a possible result of offering very little to very few?

When you focus, you define what you do and for whom you do it. This is a narrowing process. And it's one of the best ways to ensure your entire organization is working toward a common goal. Take King Arthur Flour as an example.

King Arthur's business focus is producing very high-quality baking flour for educated consumers. It's not really in the flour business as much as it is in the baking business. This simple focus motivates employees because they know their products are being counted on to make the customers' baking experience the best it can be.

King Arthur uses its focus to distinguish itself from the competition as well. This business focus helps the company earn the respect of its stakeholders. Both the leadership and the workforce feel that King Arthur is special because of what it stands for, what it does, and how it does it.

Focus is probably one of the most difficult concepts for many leaders to accept. We often equate focus with limitations or saying no to opportunities. To most people, saying no to opportunities is like saying no to growth. But focus does not mean giving something up. It means identifying your company's claim or promise—the benefit you promise to deliver to your customers each time they buy from you.

In *The Long Tail*, Chris Anderson reminds us of the power of focus. "The long tail" is the name for a well-known feature of some statistical distributions. In long-tailed distributions, a high-frequency population is followed by a low-frequency population, which gradually tails off. The events at the far end of the tail have a very low probability of occurrence.[1] The theory of the long tail suggests that businesses can shift from a focus on the mass market at the head of the demand curve and toward a huge number of niches in the very long tail.

So what does this all mean to your business? It means that instead of wallowing around in the undefined majority, you must focus like a laser on the niche market segment that is really interested in buying your product or service.

It is simply impossible to be all things to all people and have a realistic, meaningful claim. In order to devise an effective and realistic claim or promise, you must focus. Fortunately, we have a number of very good examples of companies that know how to focus. For example, Google promises to focus on the user, and all else will follow. FedEx promises overnight delivery to people who want to pay a premium price for it. Whole Foods promises to set standards of excellence for food retailers. Nordstrom and Four Seasons Hotels and Resorts attract upscale customers with their customer service promises, even with upscale prices. Southwest Airlines promises low fares to those who don't care about an assigned seat on the plane. In every case, these companies focus on a target market that values the organization's promises.

Another way to look at your business focus is to equate it with your business purpose. Once you identify your claim or promise, it becomes the purpose of your business. It's the rallying cry for everyone working in the business. Simple promises like great coffee, the best customer service, and the lowest prices become the yardsticks by which people in the organization measure their own contributions. If they further the purpose of the company by their actions, they are contributing. If not, they had better change what they are doing.

Executives need to know the business purpose of their company. Too often, leaders are afraid to start talking about the company's purpose because they may exclude a stakeholder or a customer. They are afraid it will frighten the herd! However, once they begin to really understand the purpose of their business, it becomes easy to translate that value into a higher purpose. It makes it easier to define the operational elements employees do every day that are aligned with that purpose.

So how do you identify the purpose of your business? It starts with understanding the needs of your customers.

Know Your Customer Niche

Business opportunity is found at the intersection of changing customer needs and entrepreneurial perspective. Changing demographics, technology, regulations, and even changing geopolitics affect your customers. As a result of change, customers become disenchanted with the status quo. They begin to consider new products and services that can improve their situation. For example, consumers have less free time, so they look for time-saving products and services. Their budgets are tighter, so they look for value. They are more concerned about their health, so they look for health-oriented products. Corporations affected by stiff competition or a downswing in the economy look for money-saving ideas. Companies affected by changing regulations look to protect their market positions or capitalize on new opportunities.

Customers make a *decision* to buy from you. They have gone through a process of determining that what you're offering best meets their changing needs. This process is normally informal and often occurs at the subconscious level, but it's important to understand.

If you assume customers buy from your organization just because there is a demand for what you offer, you are treading on thin ice. In the best case, you miss the opportunity to understand what customer need your offering fulfills. In the worst case, you ignore warning signs that may indicate your customers are about to shift to a competing offering that better meets their changing needs.

Have you stopped to think about what *changing* customer needs you address with your product or service? Do you understand why your customers buy your products or services? Is your business addressing their need for lower costs or are you saving them time? Does your product or solution offer new capabilities that will help them maintain their market share? Are you offering an incremental improvement to a recurring operation?

Spend significant time answering these questions. Seek the opinions of other people in your organization. Ask your customers directly. Study your competitors, and ask the same question about their products and services.

Analyze your current customers and identify the issues facing them. Once you do this, you can identify how your products or services uniquely fulfill the changing needs of the customer. Engage your entire organization in answering these questions:

- How can we describe our customer niche?

- What concerns do our customers have?

- What challenges are they overcoming?

- Are they trying to lower their operating expenses?

- Are they more concerned about revenue growth?

- Are they facing new competitors?

See if you can categorize current customers by the issues they face. Conversely, you can categorize current customers based on the primary benefit received when they purchase and use your products or services by answering these questions:

- Does our product save our customers time?

- Does our service save our customers money?

- Will the purchase of what we offer to customers increase their effectiveness, efficiency, or productivity?

- Does our service create an additional feature or new functionality for our customers' products and services?

- Will they gain any personal benefit from purchasing our product or service?

An intimate understanding of the issues facing your customer base and the benefits your products and services afford them will allow you to identify every customer in your niche. Then, your organization can discuss what claims or promises need to be made to each of the customers in this niche.

In order to serve and perhaps even dominate a niche, you must make sure every component of your business focuses on that niche. There must be alignment of that market focus with every corporate process throughout the product or service life cycle, as well as a shared purpose among the company's internal stakeholders.

Understanding the niche or niches your customers occupy can help you serve and potentially dominate that niche. A focus on the niche gives you an opportunity to target specific needs of specific customers. It forces your business to align its policies, processes, and structure toward the single goal of dominating the niche.

Rich Gergar of G&G Outfitters exemplifies exceptional niche focus. He demands his leadership team step into the shoes of their customers and answer the question, "What does my customer need?"

But not every company does this, and many struggle with the idea that they should focus on a niche. Their executives have developed a scarcity mentality. They believe that if they don't scoop up every piece of revenue, regardless of whether it makes sense for the company, they're going to starve to death. They get used to trying to sell anything to anyone.

By contrast, an abundance mentality means focusing on a niche and dominating it. Companies that dominate niches have a much easier time aligning their core processes to their customers' needs.

Responding to New Niches or Shifting Niches

If you understand your niche, you'll also understand the trends affecting the niche. Understanding the trends will keep you one step ahead of the shift. Consider the member management software market niche. This is the segment of the software market that serves any organization that tracks its members.

For years, a number of successful software providers served their market by building high-quality software that tracked members for trade associations, churches, or civic groups. However, this market has been recently hit with the perfect storm of market conditions and customer needs. First, proprietary member-management software products took on newer and cheaper competition from both open-source providers and companies that provided the same functionality in less-expensive software. To add insult to injury, the user base began to dry up as consumers saw fewer and fewer reasons to join traditional associations when they could get the same benefits from social networking sites like LinkedIn or Google Groups. Fee-paying member-based organizations found their membership dwindling, which resulted in lower revenues and less investment in member services. Just at the time they needed to find ways to be more competitive with free services like LinkedIn and Google Groups, these organizations had few resources to invest.

Consider also the marketing and communications company that leveraged its skills and competencies in logos, branding, and print media to become a Web design company. That Web design company then observed the shift in the tools available to build Web sites and began shifting toward Web-based application development. When the company saw a trend in this kind of work being shifted to overseas providers, it leveraged its business knowledge and shifted once again to become a consulting firm staffed with business analysts providing a service and acting as intermediaries between the customer and the overseas technology service provider. Three significant shifts over a ten-year period allowed the company to survive and prosper.

Whether your company can successfully transition its products and services from a dying market segment to a prosperous market segment during times of change takes more than business focus. It also depends a great deal on the viability of the company's financial model.

Financial Model

The financial model is a dashboard that shows how well the company is doing and how well the company tracks its progress. Both elements are critical. It's one thing to know your company is performing below expectations; it's another to know why you are doing well. All large companies and even most midmarket companies use a dashboard to identify their key management indicators. Think of this dashboard as a scorecard or a health checkup for the business.

Ideally, your dashboard should focus on leading indicators since they will provide the leadership team with the most insight into future operations. Lagging indicators are generally the norm, and although they are "rearview mirror" statistics, they provide the leadership team with insight and trends. When used in conjunction with forecast and modeling applications, they provide an excellent management tool.

To prepare a list of indicators for your company, there are two questions you should ask yourself. What information do I need to understand how my business is performing? What are the critical success factors of my business? The answers to these questions are your key management indicators. If you want more guidance, obtain the annual reports of your publicly traded competitors. They will be chock-full of key management indicators.

Here are some key management indicators of a service company. Each of these indicators represents a component of the financial dashboard of the company:

- *Revenue*—Sales of products and services measured in dollars
- *EBITDA*—Earnings before interest, taxes, depreciation and amortization
- *Turnover*—Churn rate measured as a percentage of the workforce
- *Hires via referral*—Percentage of employee-referred new hires
- *Business development pipeline volume*—Dollar volume of forecasted business opportunities
- *Customer satisfaction*—Customer perception minus customer expectation
- *Employee satisfaction*—Results of annual employee survey
- *Profit per headcount*—Gross margin per employee
- *Open requisitions*—Number (percentage) of current staff openings
- *Contract backlog*—Dollar volume of unfinished work under contract
- *Project profitability*—Gross profit margin of each project
- *Overhead rate*—Indirect costs associated with running the business

- *Division profitability*—Gross margin on an aggregated book of business

- *Gross margin*—Profit rates associated with direct labor

- *G&A rate*—General and administrative costs as a percentage of revenue

- *Multiple*—Multiplier for direct labor equating to the total cost of service delivery

- *Cost per hire*—Total cost of hiring one new staff member

- *Days revenue outstanding*—Elapsed time to see revenue after work is billed

- *Available cash*—Amount of cash available for operations

- *Prime contracts*—Percentage of revenue from primary contracts with clients

- *Subcontracts*—Percentage of revenue from subcontractor relationships

- *Résumés in pipeline*—Number of identified candidate résumés available for interview

If you can identify your key management indicators, you will have a good understanding of the financial model of your business. You can identify the factors that control profits, such as low operating costs, high prices, or sales volume. And you can set specific targets for the operational performance of your business, for example, keeping employee turnover under 15 percent or generating $100,000 in revenue for each employee on the payroll. You can develop management reports that track this information periodically, and you can share it with your leadership team and perhaps even the entire company. Then, be sure to stay on top of these key management indicators.

Establish reasonable targets for your key management indicators based on your understanding of how your business operates. Then, determine how you stack up against those competitors. Realistically determine if your business will be able to compete economically with competitors. For example, if your overhead costs are 25 percent of sales and your competitors' overhead costs are 18 percent of sales, you have a problem.

Another important aspect of your financial model is the treasury function of the business. Standard accounting ratios such as debt to equity, return on equity, return on assets, profit margin, or current ratio—the ratio of current assets to current liabilities—are obviously important to the chief financial officer, but front-line managers also need to understand these more complex financial relationships in order to have a positive impact on them. For example, asking a front-line manager to reduce expenses for a period of time is easier if the manager has a general understanding of the bank covenant that requires the company to have a certain amount of cash on hand at the end of each quarter in order to retain favorable lending conditions. Set targets for each of these ratios based on industry norms, then track your performance against those targets.

Additionally, you should identify the major components of your cost structure. On what do you spend your money? Is your business capital-intensive? Is it people-intensive? Do you have a high percentage of fixed costs such as salary? Can you turn fixed costs into variable costs through outsourcing? Perhaps you can outsource your accounting department or your information systems department and lower your fixed costs. If you have an operating budget, review the major cost categories.

Finally, consider the price of your products or services. How do customers pay for the value you create for them? Will your customers pay the price you need to charge? How do your competitors price their products? Could you price your product differently and gain a competitive advantage? The cost represents your understanding of what it takes to deliver a product to your market, but it is equally important to understand what price the market will bear.

Your key management indicators, your accounting ratios, your cost structure, and your pricing strategy represent the economic model of your business. If you are the manager of a unit within a large company or even the leader of a team, it is important to develop your own key management indicators. Your organization probably has developed these indicators for the business as a whole, but don't rely on them alone. Develop your own indicators and targets that apply to your corner of the world. Establish management and reporting systems to gather this information on a regular basis. Make business decisions with your economic model as a guide. Innovate every chance you get. The profitability of your business depends on it.

Operating Parameters

The next element in your business model is the business operation. If you took a snapshot of your company or your business unit or division right now, what would it look like operationally? How many employees do you have? How many office locations are there? How many products do you offer? Who are your competitors? How do you distribute your products? And what will your business operation look like one, two, or three years down the road?

Your operating parameters define the operating reality of your business. They define what your vision really means operationally. If your vision is to become a $500 million business, your operating parameters define how you intend to get there. Will yours be a regional company, a national company, or an international company? What percentage of revenue will come from existing customers? What percentage of revenue will come from existing products and services?

It's critically important to build a broad consensus regarding your business's evolution. Without a consensus it is difficult to develop coherent strategies to support your goals. For example, people will disagree on the direction of the business. Some may believe that to get to $500 million in revenue you have to open new offices in other cities. Others may believe developing new products is the key. And still others may believe you don't have to change a thing to get to $500 million in revenue. Which path do you choose?

Buying into the Vision

Building consensus on the operational reality of your organization won't happen by itself; it will take leadership on your part. John Kotter of the Harvard Business School defines leadership as a three-part process: establishing a vision, creating alignment, and motivating and inspiring. Creating a vision that can be operationalized is part one of that three-step process. The "Mount Sinai approach," coming down to the people with the two tablets, won't work in today's world. People must be able to identify with the vision. The best way to make a vision inclusive is to have involved people in its development.

Organizations often struggle to get a shared vision of where they are headed. The benefit of going through that process—and it doesn't have to be a struggle—is that it adds clarity to the values of the company. The process also defines not just where you're going but how you'll get there, and it is grounded in your company's values and culture. Clarifying the vision, values, direction, and culture of your company is crucial. Not everyone may define success in the same way, but your company needs to define success in one clear, consistent fashion in order to have everyone on the same page.

Building consensus on the operational reality of your organization won't happen by itself; it will take leadership on your part.

At a minimum, your leadership team needs to understand the company's core values and competencies and exactly how the company is capable of going forward. The vision needs to be stretched far enough into the future to get everyone excited without being far-fetched. Encourage your leadership team to stretch their thinking, but at the same time, remember to involve some aspect of practicality. However, at this point, if you have to choose between stretching and being practical, favor the stretch.

How do you know you've succeeded in creating a shared vision? Ultimately, when you present the new vision to the next-generation employees at an all-hands meeting, and they are all on board, you know your vision is on target. The worst situation is when you first articulate the new vision and you get a collective rolling of the eyes. In that case, you know it didn't work. The vision was a little too grandiose, a little too impractical, and you have to dial it back a bit. The vision you construct must be based on some sort of reality and not just wishful thinking. Start communicating the vision early and do it often. Mac MacLure, CEO of RWD, meets with all new employees during their orientation to present RWD vision, describe the company's plan, and administer a "strong dose of culture."[2]

To achieve not just a workable vision but also buy-in for the idea, the entire leadership team must be involved in its conception. The collective wisdom of the entire team will create a possible, practical vision of where the organization can go. It's important to make sure one egotist isn't dominating the conversation, grandly announcing "We can do this!" when nothing in the company's history indicates it's possible. It's also important to make sure a diverse group of people are behind the ideas being promulgated. Otherwise, a big chunk of the team will be alienated.

Creating the Vision

The process by which the vision is created begins with one question: what will the organization look like in the near to not-too-distant future? As your team works on the answers, have them think two to five years out from today.

Once you begin discussing the future of the company, other questions will naturally flow from the main question.

To create your vision, begin by looking ahead for two to five years and answer the following questions:

- How do you see your job changing? (This is a question for each person on the team.)
- Who is affected by your product or service at this point and in the future?
- What are your customers doing differently?
- How has your product or service changed?

- Who is using it, and just as important, who has stopped using it?
- What new regulatory issues do you face?
- Who are the leaders in the marketplace by the future date you've chosen?
- Who's collaborating with your company?
- Who could potentially become a collaborator?
- What's the image of your company?
- What are all your stakeholders—your employees, your customers, your partners, your bankers, your prime contractors, your subcontractors—saying about you?
- Do you currently fulfill any obsolescence in the market?
- What are you doing that will go away, be done differently, be outsourced overseas, or otherwise be unrecognizably different from its current state?
- Are the Millennials, the generation born after 1984, important to you? How are you appealing to them as a service provider or as an employer?
- Do you care about your company's role in the community? Are you going green? Are you philan-thropic? What does your organization care about?
- What are your unique contributions as an organi-zation? What is your company's purpose?
- What skills do you and your staff need in the future that you don't have now?

- How have you gotten through changing times? How did you get through the downturn or recession of 2009–2010?
- How do you treat people? How do you recognize them for what they do? What are the core values of your organization?
- How do you retain people?
- What has your company done to ensure there is a legacy, a next generation of leaders?
- What goals and objectives would your team have after you have accomplished this current round of initiatives?

It's best to discuss each issue over a period of several weeks and give everyone the green light to say or contribute whatever comes to mind. As the expression goes, the mind is like a parachute—it works best when it's open. This process is all about opening people's minds to what the future can be. After each of the questions has been thoroughly discussed, give the team the following exercise.

Ask the leaders to draw a map—some sort of allegorical or metaphorical construct of what each one thinks the future will contain—on a large sheet of paper. These maps may have features like valleys, mountains, oceans, cliffs, deserts, beaches—whatever the executive wants to use to illustrate the future of the company. The maps may look extremely different from one another. Sometimes they look like the maps on MapQuest, and sometimes they are maps of the galaxy, straight out of *Star Trek* or *Star Wars*. Any concept is fine as long as it represents a vision of the key features of the organization in the future.

One CEO I knew drew a mountain on his map and depicted an individual pushing a snowball that grew increasingly larger on its rise to the peak. His point was that the snowball was going to roll, one way or the other, and both directions seemed uncontrollable. How do you get a grip on that snowball before it turns into an avalanche? That's the question he wanted to think about.

Some people hate this exercise; some love it. If you have twenty people in the room, you can break them up into teams of five. Ideally, you just want three or four maps when you're done. If a group has only two to four people, it's harder to get everyone involved because people in a smaller group often feel more embarrassed about sharing what they're thinking about. Teams of five work well, especially if there's an artist, real or self-styled, in each group.

Maintaining Momentum

Once the vision is created, you must consider how to maintain momentum while working on the infrastructure of the company. One expression is that "it's tough to work on a plane while it's flying." But then, you've got to consider the space shuttle. NASA is continually working on the shuttle, not only when it's grounded but also while it orbits Earth. This shows it is possible to make small changes and even big changes while everything is up in the air, literally and figuratively.

You want C-level executives to realize they are already paying for visionaries—they're on staff, but they may never have been listened to in the past. During a visioneering exercise I held with a midmarket technology firm, the employees were finally able to get their CEO to recognize the importance of a particular new service they wanted to offer. The team said, "We've been beating him over the head for a year trying to get him to listen!" Well, he's listening now. Whether the company is too late to market is something only time will tell, but it's a certainty that this CEO wasn't paying attention to the visionaries on his own staff.

Creating an operational vision doesn't mean battening down the hatches to prepare for a recession. It's not about looking at the next wave and figuring out what to do. It's knowing what to do with the wave after that.

Core Processes

As the leadership team adds depth and clarity to the vision of the organization, the core processes of the organization begin to become the natural enforcement tools for maintaining a certain momentum of the vision. Your business processes enable your business to operate and achieve its goals. They must be designed to support the operational picture defined by your operating parameters.

If your parameters specify that you will hire three hundred people over the next three years, you need a very robust recruiting process. If your parameters specify that you will open retail outlets across the country, you'll need strong real estate and facility management processes. If your parameters specify that you will develop several new products, your product development processes are critical. If you expect the number of customers you serve to grow exponentially, your billing and collections processes need to support this growth.

The key is to identify your core processes, those processes that must work perfectly for your business to survive. For example, if your company manufactures private label pharmaceuticals, your core processes are contract manufacturing, sales, and distribution. If your company fabricates custom steel products, your core processes are design and fabrication, sales, and delivery.

In a professional services business, like accounting and IT services, the core processes often include staffing, customer relationship management, and service delivery. That's because in consulting, success depends on the ability to have the right people available for the right client assignment at the right time, the ability to build and maintain customer relationships over time, and the ability to routinely deliver quality services. In the consulting business, these processes must work correctly or you are out of business. They are core processes.

Systematically take apart your core processes. Break them down into key areas. Identify the critical success factors that history has shown will make or break the process. For example, if you look at the design process in the custom fabricated steel business, it becomes obvious that customer requirements and product specifications play a huge role in the success of a fabricated steel design.

Similarly, the staffing process in the services company might be broken down into the following key areas: recruiting, assignment, development, and retention. In other words, the staffing process is really the amalgamation of recruiting the right people, assigning them to customer accounts where their skills are best suited, helping them develop new skills as customer needs change, and retaining the quality people on staff. In this example, history has shown that if you can recruit, assign, develop, and retain people effectively, your staffing process will operate effectively. And if your staffing process operates effectively, your business will operate effectively.

The extent to which you specify these processes will depend on your particular business. The minimum amount of specification requires you to provide simple but flexible guidelines (think recipes) for each core process. In this case, your goal is to provide insight on what has worked in the past so that other people can have a better chance of succeeding. At the other end of the scale, you can rigidly specify a process so that it becomes a repeatable, mechanical operation, like making french fries at McDonald's. If flexibility of the process is not a driving concern, a more rigid specification can provide more control. In either case, you must never allow the processes to take control of the business. You need to constantly review your processes to ensure they support your ability to create customers and operate the business efficiently enough to earn a profit.

The best approach is to pursue flexible guidelines. In the current business climate, flexibility is a critical success factor. When processes are overspecified and rigid, flexibility decreases and people depend on the process to do their thinking for them. Don't fall into that trap.

When specifying your core processes, consider yourself a painter. Imagine you are painting a beautiful mountain scene. You set up a chair, paints, brushes, and your canvas out in an open field and begin to paint. Repeatedly, you glance up at the mountain scene, focusing on a particular aspect of the scene and trying to recreate it on canvas. Studying the subtleties of the real scene, you incorporate them into the painting. You bounce back and forth between reality and your representation of reality. The real mountain scene becomes your guideline for recreating it on canvas.

This is the effect you want from core process specifications. You want everyone in your organization to look up, examine the process guidelines, and apply them to the business situation at hand. You want people to study the process specifications and recreate them as best they can in the real world of business. In painting, it is impossible to recreate reality on a canvas with 100 percent accuracy, but you can come very close. You can capture the essence of reality so that the painting truly inspires an image of the real thing. The same is true when trying to consistently execute business processes. You can't identically execute the process every time, but you can come very close. Your goal is to capture the essence of what works. When you do, your business will run like a gazelle.

Putting It All Together

Now that you understand the business focus, the financial model, the operating parameters and the core processes, what's next? How do you put everything all together into an effective operating model? The answer is leadership! It takes effective leadership to ensure that everyone in your organization can effectively execute your operating model. We'll discuss leadership a lot more later, but for now, here are two specific guidelines for turning your business design into a world-class operating model:

- Align your business constructs with your operating model.

- Analyze your operating model across your entire supply chain.

Let's look at an example that illustrates these two points.

A mother and her young son went into a department store to purchase a pair of sneakers for the boy. The salesperson measured the boy's feet to determine his shoe size and discovered that his left foot was a half-size smaller than his right foot. Although it's very typical for young children to have different-sized feet, the salesperson's response to the situation was atypical.

Instead of fitting the boy with a pair of shoes that fit one foot well and the other foot poorly, the salesperson took a different approach. He went to the storeroom and brought back both a pair of size 12 sneakers and a pair of size 12½ sneakers. Breaking the pairs of shoes apart, he offered to sell the woman two different-sized shoes so they would fit the boy's feet better. Now that's customer service!

Can you guess which department store this was? You got it! It was Nordstrom.

Nordstrom is famous for its attentive customer service. In fact, Nordstrom's mission is to be known as the department store with the best individualized customer service around. That's its business focus. Its advertising and marketing activities constantly reinforce this customer-focused image. But image and words are not enough.

A company's image must be based on substance. Eventually, a company's operating model must be designed and calibrated to support the marketing image that depicts the company's business focus. Otherwise, any claims will seem shallow and empty. Let's go back to our Nordstrom example to better illustrate our point.

Think about this seemingly trivial action of selling two different-sized shoes for a moment. Without a well-designed and thought-out operating model, the salesperson would never have acted this way. He had to be trained on how to be attentive to customers, even young boys with two different-sized feet! He had to be empowered to make this decision on the fly. And the store's core processes had to accommodate this situation.

When that salesperson took two pairs of shoes from inventory, sold one pair, and failed to return the other pair to the inventory, it set off a chain reaction of events that profoundly impacted the store's business systems. The store had to send the mismatched pair of shoes back to the manufacturer and receive credit. Therefore, it needed a contractual arrangement with the manufacturer that allowed the store to return shoes when it sold only one shoe out of the pair. The inventory system had to account for the possibility that more than one pair of shoes might be needed to fulfill a customer order. Otherwise, inventory levels could be understocked even though sales levels were accurately predicted. The salesman's commission had to accurately reflect the fact that he sold only one pair of shoes, not two. The quality control systems had to be flexible enough to recognize that the shoes weren't defective, even though they were returned to the manufacturer for a credit.

Virtually every business system within the store was affected by this one simple action of selling two different-sized shoes.

As this story shows, it's one thing to define attentive service as your business focus; it's another thing to build an operating model that guarantees that the business provides attentive service. Remember, to be different today you have to act differently. Your operating model determines how you act. The model has to support and enhance your vision for the business. Therefore, every aspect of your business operations must be choreographed to support and enhance your business model. Otherwise, your operating model will be working against the achievement of your business vision.

Your operating model consists of the processes, procedures, and systems that span the entire supply chain of your business. It's not enough to reconfigure your operating model. In many cases, you have to reconfigure your interface with suppliers, partners, and customers as well. Keep in mind that sometimes suppliers are so powerful, you have to build your operating model around theirs.

In many cases, your suppliers build their operating models around their view of your business methods, much like carpenters and bricklayers working for a builder. That's why you have to have a very broad perspective when designing your operating model. Otherwise, the side effect of seemingly innocuous decisions can have a profound impact on your business.

Your operating model can be viewed as the physics of your business. And you can't fight physics! All the good intentions and powerful words in the world won't overcome an ineffective operating model. Your operating model will determine how your business behaves, whether you like the result or not.

Whether you are part of a larger Fortune 100 company or the leader of an entrepreneurial start-up, it's critical to get your operating model right. It has to support and enhance your vision for your business as defined by the business focus, financial model, operating parameters, and core processes. You start with a vision, but you bring it to life through the operating model, which is the soul of your business. It is the character of your business and supports your company's public image or personality. And it manifests itself in the perceptions your customers have about your business.

Conclusion

Your business capitalizes on an opportunity found at the intersection of changing customer needs and new business approaches. It challenges the status quo in your industry so you can discover a better way of operating. It identifies a niche market to which you can lay claim. It differentiates by narrowing your focus. It designs your business to fulfill your vision.

The perspective provided in this chapter will help deconstruct your business and examine it from the viewpoint of an entrepreneur. It will help you craft an operating model that supports your business vision. The goal is to ensure the entire organization works toward achieving your business vision.

Practically speaking, you won't be able to stop doing what you do every day and sit down to redesign your business. You have to keep feeding the troops even while you consider a new strategy. But, you also need to carve out significant quality time to think about your business using this framework. Start by formalizing your core processes. That way you'll receive immediate tactical benefit. However, you must eventually engage your organization in an open debate about the entire operating model, starting with your business focus.

Identify the good ideas floating around your organization. If you decide to change directions or narrow your focus, start slowly. You need to manage your current business so you can maximize its ability to produce a profit even while you shift your strategic focus. Profits from the current operations will fund your new initiatives.

Invest in your strategic direction and stay focused. Shifting directions doesn't require extensive spending; it requires intense focus. Don't spread your resources too thin. Once you decide to change directions, put all of your eggs in one basket. Otherwise, nothing will get done. The legendary investor, Warren Buffett, believes that you should only invest in a handful of companies.[3] According to his theory, if you truly believe you picked the best companies to invest in, why would you put your money anywhere else? Take Buffett's advice. If you truly believe you have identified a lucrative business opportunity, why would you invest in anything else?

As leader of a business, your primary job is to define, review, and challenge your operating model. But don't go at it alone. Be the leader of the process of refining your operating model, but include a broad range of people in the discussion. You don't have all the good ideas in your company! The people closest to the customer have great ideas. Your role is to ferret out the great ideas and integrate them into your operating model.

Your operating model is a central component of your Internal Franchise. This model will help teach your employees about the business. Your business focus describes the customer needs you fulfill through your product focus or operational focus. It defines your business opportunity. Your financial model determines whether the business opportunity is worth pursuing. It guides you when you make business decisions. Your operating parameters specify the business you are building. They keep everyone focused on the end goal. And the core processes bring your business to life. Everyone needs to understand the processes that are central to your business.

When your operating model is well-defined, you can turn to your employees as entrepreneurs and ask them to run it. Release the power of your people and watch your business profitably grow. Your culture will provide the motivation and reward. Your operating model is the recipe for success, and your people are the last untapped distribution channel for your products and services.

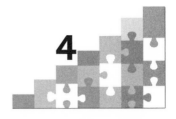

Finding Engaged
and Entrepreneurial
Employees

IN CORPORATE WORKSHOPS, I often group participants into teams and ask half the teams to answer the question, "What words would you use to describe the attributes of one of your most valued colleagues or most trusted employees?" The other half answers the question, "What words would you use to describe the attributes of a typical entrepreneur?"

Each team answers its question in isolation. Then, the two teams compare results. It's uncanny how often the lists are nearly identical. The attributes they ascribe to their most valued colleagues or their most trusted employees match the attributes they normally ascribe to entrepreneurs, with the exception of "risk taking," which we'll look at later in the chapter. In essence, participants report that their most valued colleagues or most trusted employees are entrepreneurs!

If I asked you to list the attributes of a valued colleague or trusted employee, what would you come up with? My bet is your list would include some of the following attributes:

- Completes projects

- Is honest

- Is trustworthy

- Is customer focused

- Is engaged in the company

- Has excellent problem-solving abilities

- Exercises initiative

- Is decisive

- Is accountable for results

- Is competent

- Challenges conventional wisdom

- Understands the big picture

- Is confident

In short, our most trusted employees are competent in their fields. They exercise initiative, accept responsibility for their actions, and focus on the customer. In a word, they are engaged!

So what about risk taking? Why is risk taking the only attribute normally ascribed to entrepreneurs that is not ascribed to valued coworkers? Most people associate entrepreneurs with risk taking, but when pressed to define risk in this context, they are more comfortable with the phrases "managing risk" or "calculated risk." In other words, entrepreneurs take risks but are not careless. They are prone to action, but they normally find a path that balances the risk and return.

Since we want engaged entrepreneurial people working for us, where do we find them? Are we simply lucky if they dominate our ranks, or can they be grown? Is entrepreneurialism another one of those nature-or-nurture dilemmas? Is it possible to attract and hire people full of entrepreneurial spirit? Can we be proactive in creating an environment that encourages entrepreneurialism? The rest of this chapter is devoted to answering these questions. We will examine the hiring process to ensure you are selecting entrepreneurial people and look at some common hiring issues you will encounter along the way. Finally, you'll find the answer to the question, what about those people on my staff who just don't want to be entrepreneurs?

Employee Engagement

Let's start with engaged employees. Engaged employees feel a real, personal connection to their company. They have a direct effect on productivity, so it's important for leaders to understand the factors that help build engagement and identify the barriers that stifle it. In service industries, engaged employees can make all the difference with customers. Manufacturing companies are unlikely to produce quality products without the full commitment of engaged employees.

So what does it mean to be an engaged employee? Engaged employees know exactly what is expected of them. They are crystal clear on the behaviors accepted and the results anticipated.

Creating engaged employees means changing people's behavior. Is it possible to change somebody's behavior? Certainly, if you exert pressure and threaten punishment, it is possible to force someone to act differently, but the effect is only temporary. To get people

> Engaged employees feel a real, personal connection to their company.

to change from the inside out, you must start with changing their attitudes. People change their behavior only when their world-view changes. This conversion occurs over time when it is fed by positive stimuli and allowed to take root in a new environment.

So what comes first, the change in attitude or the change in the workplace? Motivational sales guru Zig Ziglar would say, "Your attitude, not your aptitude, will determine your altitude."[1] In other words, change your attitude, and you'll do great things. Jimmy Buffett, on the other hand, might suggest a change in the workplace (or a "change in latitude") will bring about the necessary change in attitude.[2]

The normal change process goes something like this:

1.   People accept a new idea as appropriate and possible.

2.   Their attitudes change.

3.   Their behavior changes.

It all starts with the acceptance of an idea. But what change will happen if an idea is not accepted?

The Power of Attitude

Until people accept a new idea as appropriate and possible, their attitudes won't change. And until their attitudes change, their behavior won't change. They may fake the behavior if it's in their best interest, but the change won't be meaningful or lasting.

We've all seen this type of change. The boss demands change or else heads are going to roll! For a while, people make cosmetic changes that imply acquiescence to the new mandate. But over time, and sometimes it is shockingly short, their behavior slides back to the earlier state—in fact, it often becomes worse. People's behavior never really changed because their attitudes never really changed. And their attitudes never changed because they never thought the new mandate was a good idea.

Attitude is a predisposition or a tendency to respond positively or negatively toward a certain idea, object, person, or situation. It influences people's choice of action and their responses to challenges, incentives, and rewards. A person's attitude comprises two areas: emotions and beliefs.

Can attitude impact company performance? You bet! In *12: The Elements of Great Managing*, authors Rodd Wagner and James Harter surveyed 125 organizations in an attempt to match employee attitudes with company performance. The survey found that in companies where employees felt they had the opportunity and tools to do their best and believed their fellow employees were also committed to quality, profitability was 12 percent higher than in those companies whose employee attitudes were found lacking.[3]

Wagner and Harter found that employees need to feel as though they have the opportunity to do what they do best every day. This is especially true for younger workers, the Millennial Generation, who have developed a loyalty to what they do before anything else.[4] Employees also need to believe that their opinions count, that they can act, and that those actions affect the performance of the company. Finally, when employees sensed a direct connection between their work and the company's mission, the company was more profitable.

Finding people with these attitudes isn't as hard as it might seem. In fact, most people are eager to act like entrepreneurs. However, insecure leaders often stifle entrepreneurial spirit through restrictive policies and procedures. They neglect to talk to their employees about such spirit. Therefore, the concept will be new to the people you seek to hire. But the potential is there. The profits are there. Devote yourself to tapping that potential. And it starts with your hiring process.

An Entrepreneurial Hiring Process

Most hiring processes are biased toward identifying a skill match. Companies spend a great deal of time grilling employment candidates on specific issues such as their years of experience; their credentials; and their technical ability in areas such as sales, management, technology, and operations. When they find someone with a solid set of skills, they hire that person. But what about attitude? What about cultural fit?

Consider the case of Barbara. Barb is a top-notch financial type. We worked together while she was chief financial officer for a midmarket software services company. Smart, organized, analytical, proactive, and results oriented, Barbara also understands the mission of her company. She has just about all the entrepreneurial attributes you could want in a CFO. When deciding to look for a new opportunity, she found herself in a bit of a pickle because she did not have experience in one financial software application prevalent in her market. Company after company passed on her because headhunters, recruiters, or human resources departments were unable to see past this gap in her résumé. Barb eventually landed in a terrific spot, but think about all the companies that found someone with the perfect résumé but missed out on all the critical cultural attributes Barb had to offer.

Top companies realize cultural fit is just as important as specific technical or professional skills. They take extraordinary measures to attract and identify the rare individuals who will strengthen their teams. Extensive screening, although time consuming, is worth the trouble.

Over the past twenty years, I have been personally involved in hiring over five hundred people. As I look back on my successes and failures during this time, one point stands out: involuntary turnover is rarely the result of a person's inability to do the job. In my experience, firing someone was the result of either an economic change of fate or a violation of a corporate principle or value. Voluntary turnover was normally the result of a cultural mismatch. It was almost never caused by an inability to perform. In hindsight, this only makes sense. Since we had good engineers hiring other engineers or good managers hiring good managers, we successfully identified prospective employees with solid technical and managerial skills. That was never a problem. Even when people's skills weren't up to par, if they were a good cultural fit and had the right attitude, we could help them improve their skills and become fully productive. However, trying to keep someone with weak skills and a cultural mismatch was always futile.

Focusing on a skill match during the hiring process is misguided. Instead of looking for someone who has experience managing the northeast sales territory, for example, hire someone who has an inherent understanding of managing a sales force, who knows how to solve customer problems, and who accepts accountability for every business decision she makes. Instead of screening applicants for specific Java Platform skills, look for someone with a solid understanding of software development, a curiosity for the technology at hand, and a desire for responsibility. Focus on finding businesspeople with an inherent aptitude for the job and not just the perfect skills match.

Analyze your hiring process. It should accomplish three goals:

- Qualify the candidate

- Assess the candidate's cultural fit

- Educate the candidate

Let's look at these components in more detail.

Qualify the Candidate

Most of us are familiar with the first step. You invite candidates in and interrogate them on their skills, background, credentials, and expertise. Unfortunately, this step gets overdone. Employers spend too much time screening for specific skills and leave little time for assessing cultural fit and educating the candidate.

Quickly identify candidates who possess the skills you need and an aptitude for the job you want to fill. But focus on aptitude. Check the candidate's references to determine if the information on their résumés is accurate. Request transcripts and other documentation to validate their credentials. This background work should be done outside the interview. Don't waste this precious one-on-one time rehashing the résumé. Instead, use your interview time to assess aptitude. Ask yourself, does this candidate have an inherent understanding of the job we're trying to fill?

If you screen for specific leadership or management qualities, focus on behavioral-based questions. Encourage candidates to share anecdotes of how they've solved problems in the past. Instead of asking if a candidate considers himself a good leader, ask him to describe an instance when he led his staff toward a specific goal. Ask him to describe the accomplishment of which he is most proud. Does he frame the answers as an individual accomplishment or a team accomplishment driven by good leadership?

Consider using assessments to help screen for a skills match, but don't fall in love with them. Mark Ehrnstein of Whole Foods says his company discontinued using assessments during interviews because they were "not as predictive" as face-to-face interviews that documented personality traits and attitudes.[5]

Assess the Candidate's Cultural Fit

In the second step of the hiring process, focus on ensuring a cultural fit. Each time you hire a new employee, you're not only hiring someone to fill a job category or position but also making a decision to bring another potential franchisee into your organization. You're not just hiring an employee; you're hiring a businessperson—someone who can understand the company's operating model, how the company makes money, and how the success of the company is tied to her personal success. You're hiring someone who can embrace your principles and values. That is, every person you hire must embrace your culture.

As organizations build internal processes and mature, they often succumb to the temptation of allowing someone else to build their teams. In the business fable *The Five Temptations of a CEO*, author Patrick Lencioni warns leaders about abdicating their responsibility of hiring; instead, they must place an emphasis on building and eventually trusting their teams.[6]

Use the following test when adding a person to your team. Does the candidate have the ability and desire to do the following:

- Learn your operating model?

- Execute your operating model?

- Teach your operating model?

If you can answer yes to these questions during the hiring process, you are thinking in terms of attracting people with the right attitude.

A candidate's willingness to spend the time and effort to learn your operating model sets the stage for his ability to make sound business decisions once hired. If each employee understands what the company does and how the company does it, everyday actions are translated directly into top-line revenue gains or bottom-line profits. Employees will understand how

> **A candidate's willingness to spend the time and effort to learn your operating model sets the stage for his ability to make sound business decisions once hired.**

they can affect key management indicators. When executing your operating model as a part of their daily activities, they will understand the direct relationship of their actions to the success of the company. They know the decisions they make every day can materially affect the profitability of the company. Finally, when employees develop the ability to teach the operating model to new employees, your way of doing business is reinforced. One generation of employees sees to it that the next generation of employees understands the operating model, thus beginning the never-ending cycle of learning, executing, and teaching your way of doing business.

Also, ask yourself, does the candidate have the ability and desire to take these actions:

- Challenge your operating model?

- Improve your operating model?

Your competitive position is destined to change. There is certainly no sign that competition is lessening or that your products and services will succeed without changing. Customers continue to ask, "What have you done for me lately?" This necessitates constant change and improvement in your company's operating model. Just ask BP or CitiGroup about the need to adapt and change.

Spending most of your time asking candidates probing, open-ended, leading questions will help you assess their ability to fit into your culture. Consider using small teams when interviewing candidates and strive toward a conversation rather than an inquisition; people relate differently in group sessions than they do one-on-one. Ask candidates questions about their experiences working closely with customers. Determine if they are motivated to help customers. Request that they tell you stories about their experiences working in teams. Have them discuss the innovative ways they have improved their current company's ability to perform. Focus on their goals and aspirations. Are they interested in learning how your business runs? Do they take accountability for their actions? Their answers to these questions indicate how well they will fit into the business.

Educate the Candidate

Educating candidates occurs every time you go through the interview process, even if you have decided that a candidate is not a match. All candidates must leave your organization saying to themselves, "I really want to work for this company!" Just as many of us would like to own a top-of-the line Mercedes Benz, most candidates want to work for an innovative, market-leading company. Make your company the Mercedes Benz of potential employers. In this way, you become a *destination* for prospective employees.

The interview process provides an opportunity to sell your value proposition to prospective employees. Whether unemployment is high or low, all employment markets are sellers' market. Smart companies don't interview anymore; they screen, assess, and sell.

In order to "close" during the selling stage, develop a stump speech you will deliver to every prospective employee. Describe your operating model: business focus, financial model, operating parameters, and core processes. Talk about how your business expands through the concept of an Internal Franchise. Discuss the candidate's ability to be entrepreneurial.

Not every company is fortunate enough to be doing a lot of interviewing these days, but a few companies have decided to set themselves apart when closing a candidate.

Imagine you are a candidate for a key position in an attractive company and you've just gone through the interview gauntlet. On your way home, you notice an e-mail on your BlackBerry or iPhone and you decide to check it out. To your surprise, it's a video e-mail from the CEO of the company you just left. She addresses you by name, references the staff you interviewed with, and lets you know they plan on making a hiring decision right away. How would you feel? Would you be a bit more inclined to accept an offer from that company?

An e-mail like this is actually a relatively simple addition to any recruiting and interviewing process. Just prepare a short script for the CEO and set your Flip Video camera for a 10–20 second snippet. Be sure to follow a few rules regarding the message:

- Make it personal by mentioning the names of the candidate and the people he or she saw in the interview.

- Make it relevant by talking about the position and the candidate's background.

- Make it quick by posting the video before the buzz of the interview wears off.

Don't get carried away with production. We are all used to YouTube quality these days, and the idea, like most things on the Web, is to be personal and relevant.

Remember, attitudes change when people accept something new as appropriate and possible. Your first interview with a prospective employee is the best time to start explaining what is appropriate and possible in your organization. It's the best time to start affecting the candidate's attitude. You will need to spend some time explaining the specific job or role you seek to fill. Most people want to know about that. You also need to describe the basics, such as benefits, vacation time, and so forth. But spend most of your time talking about your culture. Think about how easy the interview would be if you had already made the determination that the candidate was well qualified and you were simply trying to get her to join your team. Sell your culture by truthfully making these statements:

- We are given the opportunity to do what we do best every day.

- We know our opinions count.

- We are committed to doing our best.

- We really understand the link between our work and the company's mission.

If these attitudes are in the minds and hearts of your employees and prospects, behaviors will follow, and your culture brand will be real. All prospective employees will go home or back to their friends and colleagues and say, "You won't believe the company I interviewed with today!"

Most people want to work in this kind of environment. Spend time talking to prospects about the innovative programs you have for developing leaders at every level in the company. Bruce Ballengee, CEO of Pariveda Solutions, sells Pariveda's "expectations framework" to prospective employees. He wants to make it clear from the beginning that people are expected to achieve and advance.[7] This is incredibly attractive to the kinds of people he is looking to fill his ranks with, and it scares underachievers away, which is the intended consequence.

Tell prospects about the physical as well as the intangible elements of the work environment. Explain to them the higher purpose you all share as employees of the company. When they hear you talking about it, the entrepreneur in them will awaken. Their eyes will light up. And their attitudes will begin to change. Then, when they join your company, they will be ready to be engaged entrepreneurial employees.

To compete today, you must develop a hiring process that quickly determines the level of competency and skill in prospective employees and then focuses on cultural fit. Southwest Airlines received 90,043 résumés in 2009, yet hired just 831 people.[8] The company found a quick way to assess competency and then focus on the employees who would fit the culture and add value. In the same way, your hiring process should select people who can learn, execute, and even challenge your operating model. You should focus on hiring entrepreneurs.

The Return on Your Investment

In a previous company I worked at, we invited Peter Schutz, the former CEO of Porsche, to a leadership retreat. Peter shared a number of his management and leadership philosophies, but one that hit home centered around one of his earliest decisions at Porsche. Peter had joined Porsche during a time of low profitability and even lower morale. In his first few weeks with the company, Peter met with the team responsible for entering Porsche in the Sebring auto races. During this meeting, Peter asked what Porsche's chances were for winning an upcoming race. To his surprise, the team said they had no chance. They were only entering the race for promotional purposes and to test some new technology. Peter's reaction? He proclaimed Porsche would never enter a race again except with the sole purpose of winning. He demanded the team determine how they were going to win the race. They were to come back at 10:00 a.m. the next day to explain how they would do just that.

The results were dramatic. Soon after word leaked of these meetings, Peter began receiving calls from world-class drivers from around the world who wanted to join the team now that Porsche was committed to winning. The engineering team came up with creative ways to piece parts of various Porsche models together to make a real splash in the race. High-initiative, team-oriented, and goal-driven people were attracted to the Porsche team because they sensed a change and wanted to be part of it.

In the same way, when you change your hiring process to screen for entrepreneurial spirit, the word will begin circulating in your industry. People who seek you out will be biased toward action and genuinely excited about the opportunity to work for a company that values entrepreneurial spirit. Highly competent people who have become frustrated with their current employment situation will target you as an employer of choice. Your workplace brand will start becoming independent!

Square Pegs in Round Holes

Obviously, not everyone will think this entrepreneurial stuff is a great idea. Some people just don't fit into this system. What happens to the ladder-charging, title-collecting, political barracudas wandering the halls? They'll either constructively assimilate, self-destruct, or be rejected by the cultural antibodies. In any event, don't sweat it—but don't lose your nerve, either! The corporate ladder loses its significance in a strong Internal Franchise filled with engaged entrepreneurial employees. Employees focused on the ladder are engaged but sometimes for the wrong reasons. Engaged entrepreneurial employees spend less time on the corporate ladder and more time focused on customers. They are driven by action, not corporate politics. Instead, they care about what they offer to their customers. They are so focused on keeping customers satisfied and earning a profit, they simply don't have time for petty politics.

A word about titles. During the dot-com era, the trend among the

> What happens to the ladder-charging, title-collecting, political barracudas wandering the halls? They'll either constructively assimilate, self-destruct, or be rejected by the cultural antibodies.

tech companies was to get rid of titles. Well, it didn't work. An organization needs explicit roles, responsibilities, and account-abilities, and often, titles add clarity to these. Although titles add clarity to an organization's structure, they become less significant when greater emphasis is placed on the overarching organizational success. Ideally, less energy is spent on climbing the corporate lad-der and more energy is focused on building enterprise value and serving customers. Engaged entrepreneurial employees often begin to realize that their self-worth is not wrapped up in their job title. They realize their road to success is tied to the success of the company, so they spend their time and energy on achieving that goal.

Because corporate life is different in an ownership culture, every candidate needs to be educated about your way of doing business. If people are looking to join your organization as a ladder-climbing move, they must realize there aren't any ladders to climb. Prospective employees who have spent significant time in organizations that embrace a more traditional, hierarchical career ladder are often uncomfortable with an ownership culture in the beginning. But stick to your principles. You want people to join your company for one reason: they want to act like an owner and contribute to the growth of your business.

Fallout

What about those people on your staff who just don't want to be entrepreneurs, those who have been very comfortable with the status quo? Some of these employees start out resistant to change but adapt and even grow when the environment changes and they see additional opportunities. Others are more than happy to keep their heads down and not worry about what the customer thinks. They can't imagine tying their compensation to their performance or, worse yet, to the company's performance.

Fortunately, most people respond very positively to a leadership team's efforts to increase initiative, accountability, and customer focus.

The necessity for all parts of the team to pull their weight and contribute to the overall success of the organization puts subtle yet constant pressure on everyone. Those excited about embracing an entrepreneurial spirit will succeed. Those who constantly fight the changes will ultimately be rejected by the culture. Ownership cultures have a way of keeping themselves trim. Strong adaptive cultures have built-in antibodies that over time will seek out and get rid of invaders.

You can expect some fallout when creating a workforce of engaged entrepreneurs. Some employees will be uncomfortable with the changes. Your strong culture will help filter out the few malcontents. It will also help change a few of them. Peer pressure is a powerful motivator. When employees teeter on the cusp of acceptance and see everyone else acting like owners, the urge to give it a try can be overwhelming.

Occasionally, you'll see employees who are compliant with the culture but not committed. They don't openly fight it, but they don't completely buy into it either. That's okay. Simply explain that they will be required to understand how the business works and how their actions contribute to the business as a standard part of their job. That's the minimum you expect.

Conclusion

If you are like most business leaders, you want entrepreneurial people working in your organization. Therefore, you must proactively seek them out. Devise a hiring process that assesses cultural fit. Teach prospective employees about your culture as early as their first interview, and know that some people just won't buy it. Try to identify the right aptitude and attitude as early as possible. As you insert the principles and values of the entrepreneur into your culture, some people will revolt. Don't be naïve; expect some fallout. Expect to spend significant time convincing people that it is appropriate and possible to act like an owner. Be persistent. It will pay off in spades.

Once your hiring process is calibrated to identify and select people with the right aptitude and attitude, begin to focus on your environment. If you've eliminated the excuse that you just don't have the right people but your people still aren't acting like owners, your next alternative is to look at the environment.

Hiring and firing people until you find the rare superstar won't work. Instead, create a culture that unleashes people's natural entrepreneurial spirit. Create an environment that encourages entrepreneurial employees to look for opportunities. Create hiring processes that target the entrepreneurial spirit. Capturing the lion's share of entrepreneurs will position you in a significant competitive advantage. An engaged entrepreneurial workforce will execute your operating model and make the Internal Franchise a success.

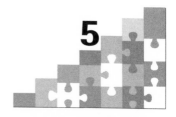

Building an Ownership Culture

ASK ANY FARMER what the key to an abundant harvest is, and he will tell you it's obeying the Law of the Harvest. He knows he must first cultivate and prepare the soil, then plant the seeds at the right time, and then nurture the crop when the first signs of growth appear. Any shortcuts will result in a less-productive harvest. He can't relax through the spring and summer if he expects an abundant harvest in the fall. Each day, he does what it takes to ensure a productive harvest. He reacts to the problems Mother Nature throws at him by relying on his experience and intuition. The farmer knows you can't cheat the Law of the Harvest.

A farmer is solely accountable for his harvest. He has nobody to blame but himself if a harvest is unproductive. He can't blame the seeds. You reap what you sow. If the weather and environment turn on him, he must react the best he can. And more importantly, he has to prepare for bad times because sooner or later, a drought will hit.

The Law of the Harvest

The Law of the Harvest is a perfect metaphor to illustrate the creation of an Internal Franchise. A critical component of an Internal Franchise is the corporate culture, which represents the franchise agreement. As we've seen, an Internal Franchise needs to have an ownership culture, which compels everyone to think and act like owners of the business. So how do you create this critical component of an Internal Franchise?

Just like the farmer, you must obey the Law of the Harvest. First, you need to define the operating model; then cultivate your corporate soil by creating an environment consistent with the attributes of an ownership culture; and finally nurture your entrepreneurial employees, looking for and encouraging any signs of entrepreneurial growth. You can't blame your employees for poor performance, just like the farmer can't blame the seeds. You reap what you sow. Leaders in this environment diligently look for signs that an ownership culture is taking root and then encourage the desired behaviors so that the harvest is plentiful.

The corporate soil is your corporate culture, and your specific words and deeds determine whether your culture is a strongly engaged entrepreneurial culture—an ownership culture. Start at the top of the organization. Identify the key management actions that will cultivate an ownership culture in your organization.

When a farmer cultivates the soil, he ensures it is rich with the nutrients necessary for the seeds to germinate and grow into healthy plants. When you cultivate your corporate soil, you ensure your culture will compel everyone to think and act like an owner. The nutrients in the corporate soil take the form of the five entrepreneurial beliefs we discussed in chapter 1:

- Belief in the leader

- Belief in the purpose

- Belief in the operating model

- Belief in empowerment

- Belief in the reward

When these five beliefs coexist, your employees will be empowered to act, and you will have an environment that allows your people to excel. This chapter shows you how to ensure that these five beliefs are operating in your company. It's not the seeds (your employees); it's the soil (your culture).

Obeying the Law of the Harvest in business means cultivating the corporate soil (creating an ownership culture), planting the seeds (empowering your employees), watching for the first signs of growth (looking for key behaviors), and nurturing the crop (providing leadership). When you follow these steps, your harvest will be abundant.

> When these five beliefs coexist, your employees will be empowered to act, and you will have an environment that allows your people to excel.

The Loyalty Effect

A common refrain among business leaders today is that employees are less loyal and more demanding than ever before. Employers complain that workers are perpetually looking for their next job, and the complaint is not far off. Today, employees always have their résumés polished. They keep their personal networks active, post résumés with online job boards, and scan the help wanted ads in the Sunday newspaper for new opportunities. But who can blame them? From January 2000 to January 2010, unemployment rose from 4.1 percent to 9.7 percent.[1] With unemployment at record heights, security is a rare commodity today.

Not long ago, workers expected lifetime employment from their employers. Corporations brainwashed most of them to believe they had few options. Society expected people to go to college, find an entry-level job, and do what they were told to do. Corporate policies and union contracts often provided lifetime employment for those people who made it to work every day on time, did their jobs, and generally kept out of trouble. But after more than three decades of layoffs, downsizing, and reengineering, this implicit employment contract has been nullified. The powerful reality of this age is that this paradigm is no longer valid.

The perceived lack of employee loyalty and commitment is a side effect of companies trying to enforce the old employment contract, even when it is obvious that it is no longer valid. When a company says to its workers, "Just do your job, and we will take care of you," the employees say, "Prove it." This isn't a sign of a lack of commitment or loyalty; it's a sign of common sense.

Employees now know companies can't and won't provide job security, and they know their career security starts and ends with themselves. They are willing to take more responsibility for their careers, but in return, they want more control over their own destinies—they want more opportunity. In fact, any company that offers job security will be viewed with skepticism. Employees know better.

In 2003, I was the COO for Conquest, a company acquired by the Boeing Company. One of the benefits Boeing was very proud of was its pension program. Senior Boeing human resource professionals were convinced that pensions more than compensated for the change to the generous 401(k) matching provided by Conquest. In fact, workers didn't have to do a thing to participate in the pension program other than showing up every day. But the Conquest workforce was populated with young, technically

ployee-employer relationship that has been characterized by
ternal competition, mistrust, and malaise.

When you stop to think about it, it's amazing that the old
del worked as long as it did. For most of this century, senior
nagement hired scores of middle managers and supervisors
watch the employees and ensure that those workers fulfilled
r end of the bargain—that they did what they were told. The
kers, on the other hand, unionized so they could keep man-
ment honest. Their union contracts ensured job security and
owing standard of living, whether or not the business climate
ne company's performance allowed it.

A changing business environment has exposed the weak-
es of this approach, but in hindsight, how could have
rican businesses viewed this environment of mutual mistrust
a effective way to operate in the first place? It's not natural.

The old contract worked in an era of high demand, limited
petition, and expensive technology because the company
in control. The consumer had few choices. In a digital era of
sparency, global competition, cheap and accessible technol-
and shifting labor markets, companies using the old model
oly can't compete anymore.

Today, the customer is in control. Consumers have all the in-
ation. Successful companies need to be fast, focused, flexible,
friendly. The current business climate demands a complete
s on the customer and an ability to change direction over-
t. Competing in this environment depends on the entire
nization working together to create customer value. Therefore,
corporate culture must motivate everyone to work together
eate value for the customer and profit for the organization.
old model of mistrust and internal competition no longer
s because it diverts critical energy and attention away from
ustomer.

savvy, and in-demand professionals who saw virt
to the pension program. They felt that either B
unable to live up to its long-term commitments
be long gone by the time a pension became part
They placed more emphasis on the opportunity
ally and professionally and preferred a 401(k) tha
able rather than a pension fund they had little c
ever manifest itself in cash payments.

A New Contract

As the old expectations of lifetime employment b
implicit employment contract has emerged. It
tunity in exchange for initiative. Employees ge
to grow professionally and personally in exch
ing initiative in creating value for the custom
the company. Their jobs become more fulfilling
and more difficult. They learn more about how
and how decisions affect the company's perfor
a more direct impact on the performance of
they have more responsibility and accountabil
mance. In return, the business seeks higher l
accountability, and customer focus from its wo
of employees changes because they now have
service level of the company is raised because
with an engaged workforce!

It's the perfect *quid pro quo*. The business
the customer is satisfied. Employees succeed
ful, growing organization creates opportunit
develop valuable business skills that will keep
in the job market. The relationship is positiv
symbiotic, and it is a noticeable departure fr

savvy, and in-demand professionals who saw virtually no benefit to the pension program. They felt that either Boeing would be unable to live up to its long-term commitments, or they would be long gone by the time a pension became part of the equation. They placed more emphasis on the opportunity to grow personally and professionally and preferred a 401(k) that was transportable rather than a pension fund they had little confidence would ever manifest itself in cash payments.

A New Contract

As the old expectations of lifetime employment have faded, a new implicit employment contract has emerged. It specifies opportunity in exchange for initiative. Employees get the opportunity to grow professionally and personally in exchange for exercising initiative in creating value for the customer and profit for the company. Their jobs become more fulfilling, more rewarding, and more difficult. They learn more about how the business runs and how decisions affect the company's performance. They have a more direct impact on the performance of the business, and they have more responsibility and accountability for that performance. In return, the business seeks higher levels of initiative, accountability, and customer focus from its workers. The posture of employees changes because they now have options, and the service level of the company is raised because its ranks are filled with an engaged workforce!

It's the perfect *quid pro quo*. The business succeeds because the customer is satisfied. Employees succeed because a successful, growing organization creates opportunity and helps them develop valuable business skills that will keep them competitive in the job market. The relationship is positive, reinforcing, and symbiotic, and it is a noticeable departure from the traditional employee-employer relationship that has been characterized by internal competition, mistrust, and malaise.

When you stop to think about it, it's amazing that the old model worked as long as it did. For most of this century, senior management hired scores of middle managers and supervisors to watch the employees and ensure that those workers fulfilled their end of the bargain—that they did what they were told. The workers, on the other hand, unionized so they could keep management honest. Their union contracts ensured job security and a growing standard of living, whether or not the business climate or the company's performance allowed it.

A changing business environment has exposed the weaknesses of this approach, but in hindsight, how could have American businesses viewed this environment of mutual mistrust as an effective way to operate in the first place? It's not natural.

The old contract worked in an era of high demand, limited competition, and expensive technology because the company was in control. The consumer had few choices. In a digital era of transparency, global competition, cheap and accessible technology, and shifting labor markets, companies using the old model simply can't compete anymore.

Today, the customer is in control. Consumers have all the information. Successful companies need to be fast, focused, flexible, and friendly. The current business climate demands a complete focus on the customer and an ability to change direction overnight. Competing in this environment depends on the entire organization working together to create customer value. Therefore, your corporate culture must motivate everyone to work together to create value for the customer and profit for the organization. The old model of mistrust and internal competition no longer works because it diverts critical energy and attention away from the customer.

A New Workplace Environment

An Internal Franchise is the primary tool to keep your company's attention on the customer. Good business leaders know the importance of staying focused on the customer, being flexible, and doing what it takes to succeed. In the current business climate, it is not enough for just the business owner to think and act this way. Everyone in the organization must think and even act like an owner of the business if it is to compete and succeed.

The good news is that an ownership culture can be infused into any business. It doesn't require new employees; it requires a change in the workplace environment—a change in the culture. The new culture must meet the needs of the new implicit employment contract. It must give the employees the opportunity to grow, and it must motivate everyone to stay focused on the customer while generating a profit for the business. In return, the employees will begin to reflect this new contract. They'll understand the constructs of the business, and they'll have an opportunity to affect the performance of the company. Employees will begin to act like owners because doing so is in their best interest and the best interest of *their* company.

Building an ownership culture is a matter of establishing a set of principles and values that encourages at the least a stewardship thought process and at best an ownership mentality. Leaders are aware of and are constantly communicating these principles and values, and they ensure that reward and incentive programs reinforce them. When you successfully combine

> **When you successfully combine the attributes of the Internal Franchise and an ownership culture with an effective operating model and entrepreneurial employees, business success isn't far behind.**

the attributes of the Internal Franchise and an ownership culture with an effective operating model and entrepreneurial employees, business success isn't far behind. Let's look at how you can create an ownership culture in your organization.

How to Build an Ownership Culture

In chapter 4, you began to view your employees as entrepreneurs. We discussed the importance of hiring people that fit the culture and about hiring for attitude and aptitude. When you embrace these concepts, you are ready to accept the central thesis of this chapter: building an ownership culture requires changing the environment in which people work. It does not mean finding new people. It's not the seeds; it's the soil.

Building an ownership culture takes a basic belief in people and a commitment to create an environment that compels everyone to think and act as a steward and even an owner of the business. Given the choice, employees want to do their best. The leader's job is to give them the choice.

Employees want opportunity. They want to be able to have an impact on the bottom line of the organization. They want responsibility and authority. They want to do their best, and they want to be rewarded for their contributions to the company's success. An ownership culture is about fulfilling these needs so ordinary people can accomplish extraordinary achievements.

Building an ownership culture starts at the top of the organization. Organizations that have the best chance of creating an ownership culture are led by men and women who value people and understand the importance of leadership. Because their hiring process selects people with the right attitude, they can commit to certain key leadership actions that will create an ownership culture.

Here is a simple mnemonic to help you remember the actions and activities that will enable you to create an ownership culture in your company. The mnemonic is TRUST:

- Teach

- Reward

- Offer Unconditional Support

- Share Information

- Be Trustworthy

Let's look at each of these components in detail so we can understand how they work.

Teach

Successful organizations share two common characteristics. First, they have developed a very effective way of operating. Second, they ensure the entire organization is tightly aligned with that way of operating. In other words, the right hand knows exactly what the left hand is doing. Let's explore why these characteristics are critical to success.

Successful companies ensure everyone in the organization, starting with the leadership team, understands how the business works. For example, Bill Toler, CEO of Pierre Foods, a $600 million food-service company in Cincinnati, Ohio, describes the most rewarding part of his job as "getting to work with everyone." Not that he spends his days making sales calls or delivering product, but his leadership approach understands and leverages the "power of influence that senior leaders have on junior people."[2] He knows he can't be everywhere, but every moment he spends with his leadership team or more junior staff can be a teachable moment. And that culture of sharing knowledge spreads like wildfire until junior staff members are thinking the same way the boss thinks! There is no better use of your time as a leader than to teach the next generation leaders how your company works.

Many companies never realize their full potential because the transfer of knowledge runs into a limited span of control. Consider a leadership team fully versed in the nuances of the business but unwilling or unable to pass that critical knowledge to second and third line managers. Fortune 500 companies flounder because even the most innovative strategies die when second-, third-, and fourth-generation leaders struggle with what it means to implement these new ideas.

Most midmarket and publicly traded companies have introduced some form of return concept into their organizations. Whether it is economic value added (EVA), return on investment (ROI), or return on invested capital (ROIC), the concept is to engage everyone in activities that have a positive impact on the company's business value.

Now, this all sounds great. No one is a bigger proponent of aligning business activity with value-added results than I am. I couldn't be happier that large companies are beginning to push these concepts deep into their organizations. The problem, however, is that concepts like EVA, ROI, ROIC, and even P&L (profit and loss) and EBITDA don't always translate well into employee actions that make a real difference to the company.

The companies that successfully implement these strategies will be the ones that can draw a line of sight between the daily activities of all employees and the indicator they are tracking, like EVA. Those that don't will be relegated to the management-theory-of-the-month club, where employees sit back and say, "If I just keep my head down for the next two months, this too will pass." The missing link between management theories and successful implementation is education grounded in a solid understanding of business financials.

To understand why many companies' strategies fail, consider what a wise (but confusing) old man once said, "What you know won't hurt you, and what you know you don't know won't hurt you, but what you don't know that you don't know will kill you." This sums up the decision-making ability of well-intentioned and underinformed employees. They are doing the best possible job that they know how to do. And if they have all of the necessary information, chances are they will make a good decision. So it's up to you, as a business leader, to ensure your employees have the necessary information and insight into your operating model.

Imagine an employee in a negotiating situation for the first time on her own. Through word of mouth, informal hallway discussions, and other indirect ways, she has discovered the company always makes money if at least a 20 percent spread exists between the bid price and the estimated cost of a product or service offering. In other words, the company's overhead and administrative costs are less than 20 percent, so the company makes a profit at a price point that provides a 20 percent gross margin on each sale.

Armed with this information and eager to get the new client's business, the employee works hard to negotiate the 20 percent margin she has heard so much about. Unfortunately, information she did not have showed she could have easily asked for a gross margin of 30 percent. The market for the product or service she was selling would have easily supported the higher price. In this situation, she missed the opportunity for an additional 10 percent profit. Did she do the right thing? Of course. Did it hurt the company? Of course. Such well-intentioned mistakes can slowly kill an organization, and they occur all the time.

An Educated Workforce

The only answer to this problem is education. All employees who have the authority to make business decisions must completely understand the company's operating model. And just as important, they have to understand how the various components of the business fit together. When marketing is battling with sales and when engineering is fighting with research and development, a tyranny of small decisions can occur.[3]

A classic example of the tyranny of small decisions is the *tragedy of the commons*, described by Garrett Hardin in 1968 as a situation where a number of herders graze cows on common land. The herders act independently in what they perceive to be their own rational self-interest, ultimately depleting their limited shared resource, even though it is clear that it is not in any herder's long-term interest for this to happen.[4]

Leaders of business units, division vice presidents, and program managers making decisions of self-interest with little regard for the health of the larger organization can turn a series of small, poor business decisions into a corporate death spiral. Leaders and decision makers must understand the fundamental and strategic assumptions underlying the operating model as well as or better than the CEO does. Midlevel executives must understand the way the company makes money and the major cost drivers of the operating model. It is the responsibility of the company's leadership to provide this education.

Whenever costs seem to be getting out of control or productivity seems to be falling, look first at how well the decision makers in the organization understand the operating model. Most of the time, underperformance is the result of ignorance, not negligence. So how do you prevent or manage these concerns?

The Failure of Command and Control

Many managers, when faced with declining performance, make the mistake of relying on processes and procedures to fix the situation. Conventional wisdom says businesses should develop new policies, procedures, and processes to control growth and manage profitability. But conventional wisdom, in this case, is dead.

A command-and-control mentality is a product of the industrial era and no longer works in the information era. Indeed, growth and profitability have never come from new processes alone. So why do so many managers fall back on such traditional constructs when faced with performance problems? Why do so many Fortune 500 executives rely solely on their monthly and quarterly management tools rather than proactively coaching and mentoring their next generation of leaders? Let's explore a couple of reasons why business leaders often react this way.

In start-up organizations, many entrepreneurs mistakenly believe the business acumen and talent of the original founders and leaders of the organization can be captured in policies, procedures, and processes. But even if it were possible to pull the business model out of the heads of the founders and design ways to implement it, a process or procedure isn't flexible enough to handle the rapid pace of change characteristic of the current business climate.

In large companies, employees still must understand their ability to impact the financial performance of the organization. It's a fate shared by both company and employee. Whole Foods, for example, has a gain-sharing program that allows teams to manage their labor budget (a huge percentage of their expenses), and a portion of the surplus is sent back to the teams in the form of an incentive.

You must be able to find a way to teach your people about the performance factors that affect your profitability. Most companies are lucky if they earn five to ten cents in profit on every dollar of sales. As a result, your margin of error is probably very small. People must perform at peak levels in order for the company to earn a profit. It's that important.

Companies competing in the digital age need a new model for dealing with a changing business landscape. The Internal Franchise model balances processes and people. Processes become tools that empowered business leaders use to provide value to customers. They are not an end in themselves. The important point is to TEACH people how the business works and how to leverage processes and procedures to work better, faster, and easier.

In chapter 3, we discussed the operating model for your business. Use this framework to TEACH your employees. Engage them in broad discussions about the business and how it works. Seek their opinions on how to make it work better. Make sure they understand the key operating specifics of your business, and then, turn them loose. Your ability to improve corporate performance depends on it.

It's All in the Game

Great leaders are great teachers, but even the best teachers need a few aids. One example is Risks and Rewards, a board game developed by Beyond the Box, Inc. Think of it like Monopoly but tailored to specific operations, business strategies, and performance factors for your business. Its purpose is to help everyone in the organization create a line of sight between their daily activities and the performance of the company. The game provides an effective way to teach key corporate concepts such as P&L, ROI, or ROIC and to let people know that their actions have an impact. A number of business simulation games are also available, and the majority focus on financial management. The interest in most of these games lies in the accurate simulation of everyday occurrences using business rules implemented in software. The best of the games closely tie the actions of the players to expected or plausible consequences and outcomes. They reinforce the idea that there is a direct connection between everyday business actions and the operational performance of the business.

It's not enough anymore to send ten executives to Harvard every year with the hope they'll expand their leadership ability. This type of professional development is important, but to have a dramatic effect on how your employees work each day, those employees must become the targets for learning. Whether you lead an organization of three hundred or one of thirty thousand, you must find a way to build knowledge workers throughout the organization who understand how their daily actions affect company performance. Build a critical mass behind your operating model by teaching everyone in the organization how your business works.

Reward

Whether you are running a Fortune 500 company, leading a $10 million business unit, or managing a five-person project, you sometimes need to remind yourself of some simple entrepreneurial axioms between business performance and personal financial success: all successful entrepreneurs understand the inextricable tie between business performance and personal success. When the business succeeds, the entrepreneur succeeds. If the business fails, the entrepreneur fails. Smart entrepreneurs stay focused on making the business successful; their personal success depends on it.

The Law of the Entrepreneur is the fundamental principle that should govern the design and implementation of your reward system. Your reward system must motivate people to stay focused on making the business successful. For an Internal Franchise to be successful, everyone must understand the link between business success and personal success, even though everyone defines success differently. Some people view success as making a lot of money. Others view success as working with people they enjoy. Some people view success as a challenging assignment or the opportunity to grow professionally and personally. Still others view success as the ability to maintain balance in their lives—the ability to go home and spend time on a hobby or with their family. No matter how people define success, they must see the connection between the success of the business and their ability to achieve their personal goals.

Reward systems must establish and maintain this connection. The way to achieve this is to tie personal compensation and rewards to company performance. For details, see chapter 6, which is devoted to the subject of devising an effective reward system.

Offer Unconditional Support

Most business leaders have embraced at least the concept of empowerment. But what is empowerment? In their book *The 3 Keys to Empowerment*, Ken Blanchard, John Carlos, and Alan Randolph describe empowerment as "a cutting-edge 'technology' that provides both the strategic advantage companies are seeking and the opportunity people are seeking."[5] It is an advantage for both the company and the employee and a perfect corollary to the Internal Franchise.

When people are empowered, they are granted authority. It doesn't mean, however, they will act on that authority. The preconditions of empowerment include the authority to act, the ability to act appropriately, and the ability to make mistakes. Employees must believe that they have the authority to act, that they have enough information and knowledge to act appropriately, and that the organization will support them when they do act. Without the presence of all three preconditions, empowerment will remain an empty promise.

If you grant authority and educate your staff, allowing mistakes is the catalyst for true empowerment—empowerment with a purpose. We all make mistakes, and we need to extend this privilege to our employees. They are empowered to execute your operating model and are franchisees of the business.

Treat mistakes as tuition payments—the cost of learning. In private life, people work hard and save their money so their children can get a college education. They pay the tuition bill each semester or each quarter because they know the importance of learning. Still, they feel the impact of the payment every time. There is a real price for learning; it's expensive.

It's no different in the business world. Learning is valuable, but it has a cost. When someone makes a mistake, money may be lost or a customer relationship may be damaged. The key is to learn from mistakes. Then, you and the employee can view the mistake as an investment, a tuition payment.

Analyze your company's mistakes as enthusiastically as you celebrate your successes. Make a rule that all major mistakes will be publicly analyzed and discussed so everyone can learn from them. Reward employees who exercise initiative, even if their actions result in a mistake. Publicly praise those employees who make a mistake and then take it upon themselves to teach others how to avoid it in the future. If you hold any kind of traditional leadership role in the company, set the example yourself.

Supporting mistakes also encourages the innovation business needs because a very close relationship exists between mistakes and innovation. Thomas Edison was quoted as saying, "I have not failed. I've just found 10,000 ways that won't work."[6] To innovate means your business can adapt. To adapt means your business can bring about the changes necessary for its products and services to serve the ever-shifting market conditions. In short, not tolerating mistakes is a huge mistake.

So the next time you slip up, let the company know about it. Publicly explain what the mistake was, why it was made, and how you will ensure that it won't be made again. Show everyone that you take mistakes seriously, that you are taking responsibility for the error, but that life goes on. Most mistakes aren't fatal by themselves; it's the repeated occurrence of the same mistake that hurts. That's where you draw the line.

Tolerate mistakes only if they were made with good intentions and if everyone learns from them. Good intentions alone aren't enough. You still need results. Everyone must learn from mistakes and devise ways to avoid them in the future. Becoming a learning organization, or learning from mistakes, only occurs if everyone shares mistakes. And mistakes will be shared only if the organization supports initiatives gone amok.

Avoid mistakes whenever possible, tolerate them when they are made, and ensure they are not repeated. This is the key to creating an empowered workforce.

Share Information

My father-in-law, Julius "Coach" Prezelski, was also my baseball coach in high school. Year after year, he would coach his team from the third base coach's box, and year after year, he would flash the exact same signs to his players in the batter's box. Whether a take sign, a sacrifice bunt, or a steal, his hand signals remained the same. His philosophy was that execution would determine success, even if the opposing team knew all the plays. Coach realized hiding information didn't make it valuable; using it appropriately made it valuable. Did this approach work for Coach Prezelski? You tell me. He was inducted into the Pennsylvania Sports Hall of Fame in 1994!

The same is true about most corporate information. Little of the information that management keeps so close to the vest is dangerous in the hands of employees. In fact, it's only dangerous when it's *not* in their hands. Unless the information is a bona fide trade secret on par with the recipe for Coca-Cola, give it to your employees and teach them about handling proprietary information. Use the rule of thumb that employees should see all information they are mature enough to handle appropriately. In other words, if employees can objectively use the information to make better business decisions, give it to them.

Open communication means open: everything, the complete picture, all the time. The only rule should be to protect the privacy of individuals. For example, don't share personal financial information unless it is absolutely critical. Control who has access to that type of information. Share everything else.

Managers often rely on several myths to rationalize the need to hide information when in reality they are just trying to stay in control through selective information sharing. Here are some of the myths and the reality behind them:

- **MYTH:** If I give employees that information, it will wind up in the hands of our competitors.
  REALITY: Your competition already has the information.

- **MYTH:** If I tell employees what we charge our customers for our products or services, they will demand a pay increase.
  REALITY: If employees are underpaid, give them a raise. Don't link the marketplace value of a product or service to the value of an employee.

- **MYTH:** If I share bad news like a decrease in our market share, it will negatively affect morale.
  REALITY: The workforce already understands the realities of the market and engaging them in solutions will go farther than denying reality.

- **MYTH:** If I show employees the income statement and balance sheet, they'll ask tough questions.

> REALITY: Educating the staff on the financial model
> of the company will give them an opportunity to make
> informed business decisions.

Let's look closely at four myths about information sharing.

Competition

The first myth is "If I give employees that information, it will wind up in the hands of our competitors."

Guess what? Your competitors already have all the information they need about you. They can get a tremendous amount of information about you from perfectly legal sources. Former employees, former partners, suppliers, and customers all are more than willing to talk about you. And because of the impact of information technology, the flow of business information is almost unrestricted.

The stock market is a great example. Companies traditionally release press statements about earnings, business strategies, and other corporate news after the markets have closed, especially if they have bad news to report. Their hope is the news will spread more slowly if they release it after most investors go home and are focused on more important matters than the stock market. But this approach rarely works today. Because of newswire services, the Internet, and other sources of financial information, all news spreads instantaneously. Companies that try to slip out bad news in the middle of the night are often shocked when they see that their stock's opening price is already reflecting the bad news early the next morning.

Adopt Coach Prezelski's attitude: it's not what you know, it's what you do with it. Don't worry about the information getting into your competitors' hands. Worry about the information not getting into your employees' hands. Your employees are the ones who are going to make the decisions that will affect you most. Give them all the information they need to make good decisions.

Prices

The second myth is "If I tell employees what we charge our customers for our products or services, they will demand a pay increase."

If employees demand more money when you share pricing information, there are two possible reasons: either they deserve it or they don't understand factors such as retained earnings, taxes, and return on investment. Don't hide the information. Share more of it so they will understand how the business operates. Explain to them that top-line revenue is far different from bottom-line profit. Walk through how one dollar of revenue flows through the business. Discuss how the investors in the business need to receive a return on their investment. Talk about how profit is used to fund expansion and growth. If they still have problems with the information, they may need more time to mature or they may have a personal compensation concern that should be addressed as a separate issue.

Bad News

The third myth is "If I share bad news like a decrease in our market share, it will negatively affect morale."

Only one thing is worse than someone who is always negative and pessimistic; it is someone who is always deliriously happy.

Businesses have good times and bad times. So as a naturally paranoid manager, one of the aspects of your business that probably worries you most is when someone always gives a rosy status report. If you report any problems, it probably means people or customers aren't involved. And what's the chance of that? Sharing only good news lowers your credibility. Besides, if a problem lurks on the horizon, isn't it better to get as many minds as possible thinking about the problem and its solution? Don't forget: the issue is never the bad news alone; the issue is *when* you hear about the problem. We can always deal with problems when we have enough time to do something about them.

As a leader, you need to make sure you are asking the questions that will solicit the good, bad, and ugly. Peter Schutz, the CEO of Porsche from 1981 to 1986, came to one of our corporate planning meetings and gave me the line "How do you know?" From then on, the way I would drill down past a smiley-face answer was to ask, "How do you know?" How are things going in the Southwest Region? "Fine, Marty." How do you know? Are we on target for the April 1 delivery date? "Yes, Mr. O'Neill." How do you know? Get the picture?

Get a handle on the status of each of your projects and share the good and the bad news as soon as you get it. Your people will respect you for it, and it will raise your credibility. Most likely, if you run into a problem, people will chip in to help; they won't run away.

Financial Information

The fourth myth is "If I show employees the income statement and balance sheet, they'll ask tough questions."

What's the real purpose of an income statement and a balance sheet? Did you say it was to get a comprehensive picture of the status, progress, and health of the organization? No. Read on, and take the test again!

If you view the income statement and balance sheet as scorecards alone, you miss a golden opportunity to educate your staff. Financial statements *are* scorecards, but you can use them proactively as tools to educate the staff on how the company makes money, what the cost structure of the business is, and how revenue and expenses translate into profit. By doing this, you create businesspeople. And who better to work for your company than solid businesspeople?

Routinely share the income statement and balance sheet with your employees, even if you lead a privately held company. Teach employees what these documents mean and how they interrelate. The employees will be pleasantly surprised, and they will make better business decisions because of what they learn. They will also ask you a lot of tough questions. Why are administrative costs so high? What goes into that bonus number? Be prepared to give simple, complete, and honest answers. If you treat every question respectfully, seriously, and honestly, your credibility will skyrocket, and your employees will become more productive.

Be Trustworthy

As a young man, I played a lot of rugby. I first began playing in my teens while living in England and then played for another twenty years. When you watch a well-conditioned and coordinated rugby team, you notice they are able to make blind passes, the equivalent of a no-look pass in basketball. Acting on a familiarity bred in practice and without looking, a talented rugby player will pass the ball to a spot on the field where his teammate will have instinctively moved, expecting the pass.

In a business setting, trust operates in a similar way. Imagine an entire organization moving at the pace of change while acting as one. Imagine a manager able to delegate a task or responsibility without hesitation. Imagine an employee able to focus solely on a project, customer, or business activity with complete trust that his contributions will be recognized and fairly rewarded. Moreover, imagine an environment where a manager doesn't have to delegate because her team already anticipated the need. Imagine an employee getting a raise, bonus, or other reward without it being the "appropriate" time, just because a manager believes it's right. This is the essence of trust in business.

An ownership culture is built on trust, and the only way to build trust is to be trustworthy first. Making and keeping commitments is essential to being viewed as trustworthy.

When we trust people, we rely on their honesty, integrity, and character. Trust is built over time as we make and keep commitments. You have to make commitments, and you have to keep them. It is no good to avoid making commitments in order to avoid breaking them. That's a cop-out.

Publicly committing to the tenets of an ownership culture is the first step. People in the organization need to hear that you are committed to teaching them about the business, that you are committed to rewarding them for their contributions to the success of the business, and that they are empowered to act on behalf of the organization. Make this commitment to everyone in the organization, and then, never break it. This is the value proposition you offer your employees.

When employees ask sensitive questions about compensation, profits, costs, or prices, give them simple, honest, and straightforward answers. If they challenge you on specific elements of the operating model or the cost structure of the business, view it as a sign of their interest and concern for the organization. And whenever you get the chance, proactively offer information about the inner workings of the business. Over time, the employees will view you as trustworthy. At that point, your ownership culture is taking root. Trust is becoming an important part of your culture.

Empowerment—a Reprise

By faithfully following the actions prescribed by the TRUST mnemonic, you will engender trust and create the conditions for empowerment. The next step is to ensure that your business processes and organizational structure support and reinforce

To create an ownership culture, take the actions prescribed in the TRUST mnemonic:

- **T**each

- **R**eward

- Offer **U**nconditional Support

- **S**hare Information

- Be **T**rustworthy

empowerment. You also need to manage empowered employees appropriately. Let's look at management first.

In order for empowerment to take hold and thrive, employees must act on their own. But ultimately, the business owner or business unit manager is responsible for the business and needs a measure of control. Balancing this dichotomy is more art than science, but establishing an effective communication and reporting structure is essential. Try this technique.

Establish specific reporting guidelines with the employees who have demonstrated the ability and maturity to act on their own. Let them know up front that managers are inherently paranoid. Whenever information stops flowing, managers begin to dream up all sorts of catastrophic situations. They think the lack of information means something has gone wrong. Let the employees know that whenever you start to feel paranoid, you are going to call or send an e-mail asking for a specific piece of information. You may ask about costs, revenue, progress against a schedule, employee morale, or whatever else is nagging at you. Challenge the employees to initiate communication with you frequently enough so they never get one of those calls or messages. This is their indication that they are communicating enough, and use this tool to ensure you have the measure of control you need without interfering with empowerment.

Experienced and successful managers often run on autopilot. Intuition and gut feelings are as important to a successful manager as specific training and knowledge are. And it is very difficult to transfer intuition. Let your empowered employees know that whenever you get a flash of insight about how to deal with a particular problem or situation, you will share it with them. Establish up front that your goal is to educate, not control. Give the employees the freedom to use your recommendations or to ignore them if they choose. But offer them anyway.

Your goal should be that all newly empowered employees succeed. Whenever you delegate authority and responsibility to others, hold yourself accountable for their success. Don't allow them to fail. This demands a lot of your time, but in the long run, it is the only way to ensure that empowerment permeates the entire organization. There is no better way to sow the seeds of empowerment than to point to the success stories of employees who have exercised initiative and been successful.

Conclusion

An ownership culture is a corporate culture based on trust. Building an ownership culture takes a commitment by management to teach everyone about the business, to reward employees when the business succeeds, to unconditionally support them, to share all information openly and honestly, and to always be trustworthy. Just remember the word TRUST. If you follow these practices, you will create an ownership culture.

The reward will be a workforce that believes in the leadership of the organization. All employees will believe in the vision and purpose of the business because they understand it. They will believe in empowerment because you've authorized them to act; because they possess the training, insight, and information to act appropriately;

and because they believe the organization will stand behind them. Finally, they will believe in the reward. They have a stake in the outcome and believe that when the company succeeds, they succeed.

Trust is possible in business today. Although it may seem unusual, it's not unnatural. People want to trust each other. If we create the right environment, trust can flourish, even in the high-stakes business world.

Those organizations that nurture TRUST by following the actions prescribed here will create a competitive advantage that is hard to beat because they will create an ownership culture.

Remember the Law of the Harvest: it's not the seeds; it's the soil. Your employees are okay. Focus on the environment. Focus on creating an ownership culture by performing the actions prescribed in the TRUST mnemonic. Cultivate your corporate soil and be prepared for an abundant harvest.

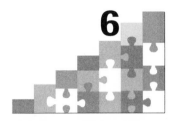

Sharing the Rewards of Ownership

SOMETHING ABOUT HUMAN nature makes us the implacable enemies of new or unknown situations. Anthropologists attribute the
situation to our status as one of the slower and smaller mam-
mals. As we evolved, our survival depended on outsmarting our
stronger and faster enemies. We developed the unique ability to
identify dangerous situations and to react instinctively based on
prior experience. We got into trouble only when completely new
situations arose—situations that required analysis, not instinct.

Another explanation is that we are just consummate game
players. If we view most situations as a game, we have a strong
need to understand the rules. Once we know the rules, we set off
to win the game.

Whatever the reason, our unending need to understand the
rules manifests itself in the business world as well. For example,
most of us behave according to the way we are measured. To do
this, we need to understand the rules of engagement within our

organization. We want to know how we will be measured and how to succeed. If the measurement criteria are not clear and explicit, we instinctively watch how other people get rewarded and strive to emulate the behaviors we believe produce the most rewards.

In other words, if leaders don't explicitly identify the behaviors they desire, employees will make them up as they go along. Therefore, it's much better to define the rules than to leave them to chance.

Business leaders, be they a founder of a ten-person start-up or the CEO of a Fortune 100 company, are constantly challenged with motivating employees to work effectively toward the shared vision of the company. They want alignment between the daily activities of employees and the businesses' goals of growth and profitability. Ideally, the employees would be aware of costs, the needs of the customer, and the opportunities in the marketplace, while at the same time finding ways to be more effective and efficient at their jobs.

But it is not sufficient for everyone to be aware of the business goals. Both leaders and employees must have a reason to reach toward those goals. And that reason is reward! In this chapter, we'll look at how to create an effective reward system for your Internal Franchise.

Humankind has been enticed by rewards since God promised Abraham rich reward for following his command. As a society, we are comfortable with a kind of covenant that links service to reward. Businesses make the covenant explicit with specific performance management programs. They have found that effective reward systems can make it easier to do the following:

- Recruit and retain qualified employees

- Increase or maintain morale and satisfaction

- Reward and encourage high performance

- Reduce turnover and encourage company loyalty

Reward systems are the critical tools that reinforce behaviors consistent with the kind of culture you are trying to create.

Autonomous, Complex, and Meaningful Work

Before we dive further into the constructs of a well-designed reward system, consider how work is performed in your company. Dan Pink, author of *Drive: The Surprising Truth about What Motivates Us*, suggests that if we really want to find a reward system that produces superior results, those in the system have to feel just the right combination of autonomy, mastery, and purpose.[1] Malcolm Gladwell, author of *Blink* and *Outliers*, points out in his stories about rice farmers in the Pearl River Delta and Jewish immigrant garment workers that work must be meaningful, complex, and autonomous in order for workers to achieve consistently superior results.[2]

Leaders are constantly looking for the "secret sauce," a compensation model that will motivate just the right behavior. They're looking for a reward system that will benefit the customer, the company, and the employee.

Leaders have to stop using old carrot-and-stick methods to motivate employees and move toward intrinsic motivators to improve performance, but finding the perfect reward system takes a great deal of effort. Rolling out an "if-then" reward system in a complex environment simply won't work. Save the if-then systems for routine and rule-based tasks. Find ways to engage employees for your toughest challenges. Remember our definition of "complex systems" in chapter 3? We said complex systems add a dimension of unpredictability to even the most complicated systems. Reward systems for complex environments must consider human nature, motivation, culture, biases, work ethic, and a host of other factors that can introduce a level of unpredictability. Let's

Consider the following questions to test whether you are engaging your workers or just beating them up with heavier carrots and pointier sticks:

- Does the workplace make sense? Does the work have purpose? Is there a higher purpose?

- Are employees encouraged to find solutions to problems? Do they feel autonomous, and are they empowered to make decisions?

- Is the work complex? Does it require higher-level thinking?

- Do employees trust that you as a leader and the company in general will stand by your commitments?

look at three factors to consider when building a reward system that matches your environment.

Appropriate, Clear, and Consistent Rewards

Work at an Internal Franchise is naturally autonomous, complex, and meaningful, but beyond the type of work performed, the reward system needs to be more explicit. It needs to be appropriate, clear, and consistent.

Appropriate

An appropriate reward system motivates behavior that is consistent with the constructs, as well as the principles and values, of the Internal Franchise. The strong culture of an Internal Franchise, an ownership culture, is driven by high levels of initiative, account-ability, team spirit, and external focus. Therefore, compensation and incentive programs must re-ward and motivate everyone to exercise high levels of initiative, to be accountable for results, to be a team player, and to focus on the customer.

Work at an Internal Franchise is naturally autonomous, complex, and meaningful, but beyond the type of work performed, the reward system needs to be more explicit. It needs to be appropriate, clear, and consistent.

Employees should make more money and have more oppor-tunity when they exhibit the qualities of an engaged entrepre-neurial workforce. The reward system must also be appropriately aligned with the organization's cultural values. Identify the values held dear by the company, and ensure any reward system meets the intent and spirit behind the shared values.

Clear

All too often, a company's reward system is its best-kept secret. For some reason, managers feel they have to control employee aspirations. Most of the time, this tendency is a side effect of a scarcity mentality. In other words, managers believe they have a limited amount of compensation to hand out, and if everyone strives to greatness, they won't have enough compensation to go around. So, the managers avoid letting everyone know how to accomplish great things.

Pariveda Solutions has developed an "expectations frame-work" that makes what is expected and what is rewarded crystal clear to employees. Pariveda evaluates each employee every six months on effectiveness, the business of information technology (the industry), putting others first, relationships and sales, and leadership. All employees know that everyone on the consulting staff has a goal to become vice president, and they know it can be done in ten to sixteen years.[3] Now that is clear!

Remember, in an ownership culture employees make decisions that materially affect the business. Therefore, it follows that if they make good decisions, the business will be successful. Following this line of thinking, when the business succeeds, there should be more benefit to share with the employees. The compensation system is self-funded by the actions of the employees.

In this environment, it makes sense to explain the rules of the game and to develop an expectations framework. If the rules of the game aren't explicitly understood, employees will never completely trust that they are being compensated fairly; it's human nature. Leaders must identify and constantly communicate the behaviors, skills, and attitudes they expect of each employee. Employees must understand that the company will reward these behaviors and only these behaviors.

Clarity also fosters open communication. When everyone knows the rules, employees feel better about openly discussing their compensation issues with management. They raise these concerns and issues before looking outside the company for new opportunities because they feel they have a basis from which to discuss their issues. They understand the rules and they feel comfortable asking management to re-address their personal situation in light of the rules. They believe they can make an effective argument as to why they deserve more money or other opportunities.

And as long as you listen, honestly consider their viewpoint, and if necessary, provide a rational counterargument, they will be satisfied. Of course, if they really are underpaid, do something about it. If you don't, somebody else will.

Consistent

Consistency is where the rubber meets the road. Imagine a situation where one of your top performers has violated one of the principles or values of your Internal Franchise. What do you do?

The answer would be easy if the situation involved a below-average performer. But what about that one guy you depend on? Perhaps everyone views this person as one of the leaders of the organization. He may have a loyal following within the organization. People look up to him.

Yet this individual has a habit of not being a team player. He refuses to help his peers, and on several occasions, he has achieved his goals at the expense of others. He has the habit of raising himself up by putting others down. He wants to become the tallest building in town, but instead of growing himself, he tears down all the other buildings around him. But he gets business results. Now, what do you do?

The answer may be obvious, but that doesn't make it any easier to implement. If your company has a list of values against which it consistently measures itself, that is a great place to start. If not, list the top five values that you as a leader hold dear. Make sure these are your five nonnegotiables—five values that if broken mean serious consequences up to and including firing. Then imagine those five values are the filtering agent for your toughest decisions. We'll call this the Values Filter, and the Values Filter is the key to consistency in your toughest decisions. Pass the questionable behaviors through the Values Filter and the right answer will become evident. It still may not be the easiest to implement and it may be the hardest to swallow, but the right answer always filters through.

Behavior–Measurement Matrix

If what gets measured gets done, then let's find a way to measure what is most important to the company's success. The best way to do this is to start with a list of desired behaviors. Following is a behavior-measurement example I have used with companies searching for ways to align behaviors with measures and ultimately personal and company goals. This approach has a significant impact on driving business results because we start with behavior, something all executives can talk about, and naturally work ourselves to measurable objectives.

Using the example of a professional services company, we started with the expected behaviors of the leaders who have a profit and loss responsibility. The following behaviors were viewed to be the most desirable for leaders with a P&L responsibility:

- Support the staff's growth objectives

- Ensure customers are raving fans

- Manage utilization

- Manage profitability

- Ensure business growth

- Ensure a successor

- Coordinate resource allocation

- Support demand creation

- Hire the best

- Retain the best

Then we developed key management indicators we felt were important to measure for these P&L managers. The following is that list of key management indicators:

- Personal utilization

- Business unit utilization

- Headcount

- Gross profits

- Completion of the talent development plans

- Account strategy

- Business unit transfers

- Completion of the next generation leader plans

- Turnover

- Customer visits

- Business unit revenues

After we identified the behaviors and the potential areas of measurement, we built a table to clarify the links between the behaviors and measures.

The power behind the behavior-measurement matrix is in the ideas being communicated. For managers with a P&L responsibility, the financial and operations standards for which they will be held accountable are now clear. It's also much easier for leaders to link the desired corporate behavior with real business results. Leaders can more easily talk about how they have to ensure their business grows (behavior) rather than a 33 percent increase in headcount (measure). It is more motivating to a workforce to hear about retaining the best (behavior) versus keeping turnover of less then 4 percent (measure). Start with desired behaviors and then work your way toward measurable business results.

The Tools of the Trade

Compensation and reward systems involve much more than just salaries. Bonus programs, health and dental benefits, vacation and holiday time off, sick leave, and equity compensation, as well as intangible benefits, are all important elements of an effective reward system. For our purposes here, consider compensation from these perspectives:

- Base pay

- Variable compensation

- Equity compensation

- Psychic income

Each of these components can help motivate entrepreneurial behaviors while meeting the diverse needs of your employees. Let's look at each of them in detail. Along the way, we will dispel some common misperceptions about how compensation systems work to motivate and reward employees.

Base Pay

Base pay is the traditional form of compensation and normally includes wages, salaries, and tips. Offering base pay as a component of a reward system is table stakes. In other words, most employees consider base pay just that, the base. Base pay normally reflects a person's role in an organization and the market demand for the expertise required to conduct the role. It is determined by the demand for what people do, how well they do their jobs, and how easy it is to replace them. Even commission sales positions usually involve a minimum base pay. As a tool to motivate employees, however, the base pay component of your compensation program is of limited value. Generally, the real value of a competitive salary is in attracting employees, not motivating or retaining them.

Your base pay structure should be a defined component of your operating model. Develop a competitive, attractive pay structure that fairly compensates people for their expertise and skill, modified by the conditions of the marketplace. Analyze your pay structure as part of defining your operating model. Avoid relying on higher salaries to motivate or retain employees. Use the other elements of your compensation program instead.

Millennials and Gen Xers

Junior-level employees, those people with one to five years of experience, are typically very concerned about their base pay. Millennials and Gen Xers entering the workforce are trying to get established. They need reliable transportation and want to pay off credit card bills and college loans. They are even beginning to consider buying their first home. Cash dominates all these concerns, so base pay plays a much larger role in motivating the right behaviors. Their focus is on improving their standard of living. They still want an opportunity for personal and professional growth, but they also want the cash! Take that into consideration when designing your salary structure. Millennials and Gen Xers should have the opportunity for larger salary increases early in their careers.

As employees mature in their careers, retirement savings, personal and professional growth, and entrepreneurial opportunities begin to play more important roles. Another 3 to 5 percent base pay increase for these senior employees begins to have less of an impact, and you can't afford to give your most highly paid people 15 to 20 percent raises every year. Besides, the more senior the employees in your organization, the more likely they will have a larger impact on the performance of the business, positive or negative. Therefore, more of their compensation should be tied to business performance.

Base pay is the foundation of an effective compensation package but it won't separate you from the competition. Base pay alone is not an effective way to motivate people. Offer a competitive salary as a tool to attract the workers you need. Once you have them on board, however, the other components of your compensation programs will need to play stronger roles in motivation and retention. That's where variable compensation, equity compensation, and psychic income (intangible compensation) become important.

Variable Compensation

Variable compensation changes, unlike base pay, which is paid in equal proportions throughout the year. Variable pay is used to recognize and reward employee contributions toward company goals, including productivity, profitability, teamwork, safety, quality, and other factors that leadership has deemed to be critical to the success of the enterprise. Employees who are awarded variable compensation have gone above and beyond their job description to contribute to an organization's success. Variable pay is awarded in a variety of formats including profit sharing, bonuses, holiday bonuses, deferred compensation, cash, and goods and services such as a company-paid trip or a Thanksgiving turkey. Unlike base pay, variable compensation is not payment for doing a job; it involves something extra.

Variable compensation is paid when someone achieves significant personal and business objectives. Therefore, it offers a unique opportunity to align behavior with performance—but only if a clear link exists between the performance of the business and the individual's contribution to the business. If that link is missing, the extra compensation will be viewed like base pay and become an expected part of the person's annual compensation. It will become an entitlement!

A simple way to think about variable compensation is to group it into three categories: incentive plans, bonus plans, and recognition plans. Incentive plans can have a short horizon like profit-sharing plans, performance-sharing plans, and individual performance-based plans. All of these can work for monthly, quarterly, and annual variable compensation programs.

Bonus plans can take all shapes. Sales and business development bonuses are probably the most common forms. Some companies use referral, hiring, and retention bonuses as a way to build their workforce. Completion bonuses, like those paid for the early and successful completion of projects, are also common.

Consider a standard bonus program. The program may be designed to encourage individual employees to accomplish specific objectives such as increased sales, customer satisfaction, or lower costs. Normally, the bonus is paid when the employee meets the performance objectives she establishes with her supervisor. But what if the business has a poor year even though the employee accomplished her objectives? Should she receive the bonus payment? If you think she should still receive the bonus, you are violating the Law of the Entrepreneur.

For a bonus program to truly motivate someone, it must be tied to the performance of the business. The bonus will be paid only if the business meets its objectives for the year, usually measured by revenue and profit targets. Once that threshold is met, then you can consider individual performance when determining whether to pay the bonus.

If you don't tie the bonus to business performance, you send the message that individual performance is more important than business performance. That's a dangerous precedent to set. What if someone offers steep price discounts in order to make a sales quota? What if someone avoids the opportunity to help the company win a large new customer because doing so won't get him immediate credit? Any viable compensation plan must first consider the behavior and then the reward.

Avoid creating a situation where people can get ahead even if the company doesn't. Make sure a direct correlation exists between the activities of your people and the objectives of your business. When personal behavior is aligned with company objectives, individual success becomes a side effect of business success instead of business success being coincidental to the agendas of individual employees, constrained only by corporate policies. Don't leave the success of your business to chance.

Use bonus programs to teach people about their ability to impact the business. Whereas salary is payment for working *in* the business, a bonus is payment for working *on* the business. Offer incentives and rewards to people that devise better ways of serving customers or figure out ways to reduce costs. Reward people for attracting new customers and new employees to the business. Use your bonus program to teach people whom everyone needs to be vigilant about identifying better ways of doing business. Teach them that their salary is payment for effectively *executing* your operating model. A bonus is paid when they improve your operating model.

The last category of variable compensation is recognition plans. Recognition plans are for rewarding the behaviors and actions that are most important to the company. Management guru Ken Blanchard and his coauthors suggest leaders stay away from "employee of the month" and become more spontaneous with "employee of the moment" kinds of recognition.[4] On-the-spot awards that recognize positive behavior immediately are very effective in promoting the strong, empowered culture that is so important for an Internal Franchise to succeed.

Equity Compensation

Companies use equity compensation for a variety of reasons. They may think it will help motivate employees to achieve their business goals. They may feel it will help in recruiting and retaining top performers. Companies may view equity compensation as a way to align employee interest with share-holder objectives. Each of these corporate objectives is probably true, but the fundamental reason any company uses equity compensation as part of a reward program is because it "gives employees a financial and psychological stake in the success of the company."[5]

In its simplest form, equity compensation means that employees own stock in the company, but in reality, equity compensation can be quite complex. Owning a stake or share of a company is a big deal, and each business with an equity compensation program should be able to concretely identify how the value of the business will increase by sharing equity. There are consequences, both positive and negative, for all parties.

When establishing an equity-sharing program, think about your objectives. If you are simply trying to reward employees, consider a variable compensation plan instead. If your goal is to increase shareholder value, then set up the plan so those people who materially contribute to the value of the company—by creating customers, reducing costs, or improving your operating model—can share in the ownership of the company they are helping to build. Tie their participation in the ownership of the company to the company's growing value and their contribution to that growth.

Don't feel that you must offer equity compensation because you think people will act like owners only if they are owners in the legal sense. It's not the case. Some people would rather not be bothered with an equity stake. And others won't act like owners even if they do own stock in your company.

You don't create owners by giving people stock; you create investors. Think about the personal investments you may have in publicly traded companies. Do you feel any sort of accountability to help the company perform? Of course, you want the company to perform; you probably demand that it performs. But you probably don't feel accountable for the performance of the business. Most of us don't even feel obligated to buy the products and services of the companies in which we invest.

Investors hold management, not themselves, accountable for business performance. Imagine your employees acting like investors instead of owners. It's the worst possible situation. They would hold you responsible for the company's performance even while they abdicated their responsibility to help the company succeed. Instead, you want employees who act like owners. The objective is to build a workforce of employees who accept responsibility and accountability for the performance of the business. These same employees will expect to succeed only when the business succeeds. These are the people you want to share in the ownership of the business.

Until you have created and nurtured an ownership culture in your business, don't even think about offering equity to employees. You need the right environment that motivates an ownership mentality first. Reward people like owners only when they act like owners. Everyone will be better off for it.

Ownership Culture and Equity Compensation

Must a culture of ownership include equity compensation? Corey Rosen, the longtime leader of the National Center on Employee Ownership and coauthor of *Equity: Why Employee Ownership Is Good for Business*, suggests that an ownership culture without some sort of broad-based equity compensation program is a bit like "being served a wonderful, elaborate dinner, but not being able to eat." Rosen suggests that "culture only" initiatives are "not sustainable for long periods of time" because over time employees will begin to feel manipulated rather than motivated. Rosen argues that a highly communicative, open-book management style, along with high involvement from the workforce as well as personal and company contributions to broad-based employee ownership plans, has the best potential for a return on a company's equity-sharing investment.[6]

The Basic Mechanics of Equity Compensation

Once you've decided that equity compensation is appropriate, you can choose one of the two major approaches to equity sharing. The first approach covers plans that are individual based, like stock grants, stock options, and stock purchase plans. These kinds of plans are reasonably flexible and can work for individuals or teams reaching certain performance objectives. Grants are probably the most flexible and can be tailored to reward performance or link leaders' compensation to the long-term success of the company. Grants either can be awarded outright or can have a restriction, like time, which would require the recipient to be with the company for a certain period of time in order to take full ownership of the granted stock.

Stock options may be the most widely used equity compensation form, and they give companies the opportunity to broaden the base of equity compensation. Stock options give employees a low-risk way of obtaining ownership since generally no compensation expense is associated with a standard option award. Many start-up and fast growing companies use stock options as a way to secure talent while holding on to their precious cash reserves.

The second major approach to equity compensation involves getting equity into the hands of as many employees as possible. Qualified employee stock purchase plans (ESPPs), 401(k)s, profit-sharing plans, and employee stock ownership plans (ESOPs) are all examples of broad-based equity compensation programs.

ESPPs give employees the opportunity to purchase company stock on advantageous terms. A link does not necessarily exist between individual performance and stock ownership and an investor mentality might trump an ownership mentality, but participation in a stock purchase plan can also signal that employees believe in the company and can indeed create an ownership bond. Generally employees elect to defer part of their base pay to the purchase of company stock. Craig McIntosh, CEO of Acrylon Plastics in Winnipeg, Canada, says, "It makes a huge difference in paying for it versus not paying for it." Craig indicated that after three years of a stock purchase program, "people stopped thinking about silos and started thinking about the big picture."[7]

Business leaders are interested in the long-term success of their companies and the best leaders place a high value on their relationships with employees. Transparency is crucial in company leadership but plays an even bigger role when equity compensation is involved. Leaders should put all their cards on the table. Be clear about the benefits of any equity compensation program you embark on, but also make the expectations and potential risks equally clear. That way, all employees can make their own decisions on the value of sharing equity in the business. Some employees will say no thanks when they finally see the big picture, while others will enthusiastically join in the risks and potential reward of ownership.

Whether the business is a privately held company or a large, publicly traded company that has a stock option or stock purchase plan, equity sharing is the ultimate form of entrepreneurial compensation. When structured correctly and used within the context of an ownership culture, an equity-sharing program can be a tremendously effective way to motivate people to act like owners and increase the value of your business while sharing the rewards of ownership. Used incorrectly, it can be viewed as manipulative and dishonest. But if you really believe in the wisdom of synergy, then an equity-sharing approach can be a powerful tool.

Psychic Income

Intangible compensation, or psychic income, is the most underrated form of compensation. The amount of psychic income employees receive from their work is the single biggest determinant of whether they will stay engaged and continue to dedicate themselves to the goals of the business.

Psychic income is the value employees ascribe to the type of environment they work in, the people they work with, the opportunity for growth they're afforded, the challenge of the job, their ability to have an impact on the business, and the recognition and support they get from the company. Don't underestimate its power. Your ability to motivate and retain the best and brightest depends on the psychic income they receive from their jobs.

> **Psychic income is the value employees ascribe to the type of environment they work in, the people they work with, the opportunity for growth they're afforded, the challenge of the job, their ability to have an impact on the business, and the recognition and support they get from the company.**

Employees want to be part of something big. They want to work with people they like, admire, and respect. They want to feel appreciated. They want to be recognized for their contributions. They want to be respected. They want challenging opportunities. They want to be able to voice their opinions on the direction of the business. They want to feel like they own part of the business—whether or not they legally own it. They put a lot of value on these intangible elements of their jobs.

To increase their psychic income, get your people involved in setting the direction of the business. Ask for their opinions. Publicly praise their efforts on behalf of the business. Look for ways to say thank you. Challenge them. Empower them. Give them the responsibility they want. Respect their talents and abilities. The value they assign to these practices is priceless.

People normally don't quit and move across the street to a competitor for a 10 percent salary increase when they truly feel fulfilled in their current jobs. In fact, most people don't like to change jobs. They like to stay put. Once you have attracted them, your strong, empowered culture offers the reason they stay. Eventually, when the word gets out, your ownership culture will also help recruit employees. Those people who want to work in an ownership culture will call you directly and offer their services. Everybody wants to play for a winner!

Psychic income is your best tool to decrease employee turnover. If your people value their roles in your company, they will stay on the job. If your people feel fulfilled by their jobs, they will stay focused on the objectives of the business.

Conclusion

Effective compensation and reward systems signal your unending commitment to creating successful Internal Franchises. Words are not enough. People behave the way they are measured. Make sure your compensation programs reward people for behaviors consistent with a culture of ownership and an Internal Franchise. Use the salary component of your compensation program to attract the talent you need. Ensure that your salaries are competitive with the industry. If you are in a competitive industry that is struggling to find talented workers, consider offering above-average salaries to attract people. Remember that younger, more junior employees will require larger salary increases each year. More senior and higher-paid workers should receive a larger share of their compensation from bonuses, stock options, and other variable compensation plans tied to the performance of the business.

Once you have people on board, use your variable compensation plans to motivate them to act like owners. Structure your bonus plans so that the business is the primary focus of everyone's activities. If you are considering sharing equity in the business, commit to sharing information, educating employees on the responsibilities of equity compensation, and involving employees so they are empowered to make decisions relating to the improved performance of the company. And offer equity only when you feel prepared to put all your cards on the table.

A carefully considered reward system is your secret weapon for your Internal Franchise. It's the reason people will ultimately stay with your company and support your objectives. With your salary and bonus plans in place, thoughtful use of equity compensation, and a focus on increasing the psychic income your employees receive from their jobs, you'll have all the ingredients for a reward system that is in tune with your business objectives. It will not only improve your business, this kind of reward system will be your most powerful recruiting and retention tool.

Engaged entrepreneurial employees want to make a difference, and when you give them that opportunity they will repay you with loyalty, hard work, and creative responses to your business challenges. Most of all, they will act like owners of your business.

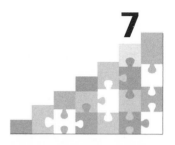

Recognizing the First Signs of Growth

HOW DO YOU know the seeds of an Internal Franchise are taking root in your organization? What should you be looking for? What are the signs that seeds are germinating, that employees are beginning to understand the operating model and feeling empowered?

Just as you can see seedlings push through the ground, signaling that the seeds have germinated, you can spot these initial signs that the operating model you've internally franchised is taking root in your organization:

- Initiative

- Accountability

- High-performing teams

- External focus

When you recognize that employees are exercising initiative, accepting accountability, working together as a team, and focusing on the customer, you can rest assured that the operating model you've franchised has a great opportunity for success.

Let's look at each of these growth signs in detail. This chapter will describe organizations where these growth signs are prevalent and organizations where they are missing. That way, you will be able to recognize their presence in your organization. Along the way, you'll learn techniques you can use to nurture and reinforce these behaviors once they begin to appear.

Initiative

Initiative falls into the category of "hard to define but you know it when you see it." High-initiative environments buzz with energy. Agile working groups spontaneously form to study a new market-segmentation strategy. Seemingly out of thin air, pilot teams volunteer to review compensation alternatives. Individual employees take action whenever something needs immediate attention. Initiatives, even the big transformational initiatives that can change a company, get moving right away.

In high initiative environments, many projects take place simultaneously. This is not to say they are well coordinated or aligned with the direction of the company, but the overwhelming urge of employees to be a part of something, no matter the size, leads them to volunteer and share their valuable time.

Most of us have experienced organizations that lack initiative. They are characterized by a feeling that the status quo is good enough. The emphasis is on the classical management activities of controlling and monitoring rather than leading and motivating. Since people in organizations lacking initiative fear the unknown, they spurn change. Paralysis sets in because everyone in the organization is comfortable with the current state of affairs.

Is initiative present in your organization? Here's a quick self-test. Ask yourself the following questions:

- Do employees take action immediately when faced with nonroutine issues that require attention?
- Are most staff members committed to growing professionally, personally, and technically?
- Do staff members feel that the leadership is committed to a growth pattern that will create opportunities?
- Do your organization's leaders normally discuss failures and look for ways to improve?
- Does it seem like new projects are always starting?
- Does the company spend more time discussing how to grow revenue rather than how to cut costs?
- Do employees generally just "make things happen" and keep everyone informed on how they went?

The more times you answered yes, the more initiative your organization shows. The higher your corporate initiative, the better your chances for getting big transformational changes off the ground.

Consider institutions like your local department of motor vehicles. These organizations seem to rely on rules and procedures more than common sense. They seem to drain the life out of everyone who works there. Initiative is usually associated with bootlickers and backstabbers. Peer pressure to comply with "the way things are done around here" is very strong. Low-initiative organizations have not established reasons for employees to exercise initiative. Therefore, employees develop a "why should I?" attitude.

Identifying and Supporting Initiative

In the book *Leadership Is an Art*, Max DePree discusses a concept he calls Roving Leadership.[1] The image of a Roving Leader captures the essence of initiative in an Internal Franchise. Roving Leaders don't walk by something that needs doing. They take action when the conference room is in a shambles and clients are due any minute. Roving Leaders don't wait to be told. They see something that needs to be done, take the initiative, and complete the tasks, because it is the right thing to do. One of the first signs of growth in an Internal Franchise is the behavior of Roving Leaders. Identify who these people are. Create a supportive environment for them. Praise them publicly for their actions, and encourage this behavior at every level of the organization.

Another sign that initiative is on the rise is a growing commitment among employees to grow professionally, personally, and technically. Whatever your industry, employees must be willing to grow, and that willingness must be supported by the organization. Corporate support can take all kinds of forms, and it doesn't need to break the bank. If employees attend a seminar or workshop, ask them to present their findings at a brown-bag lunch colloquium or an after-hours brainstorming session. If employees complete a weeklong certification program, give them a couple of days to come up with a mini-certification that the company can administer to other interested parties. Create a win-win environment for the professional development of all employees. Make sure both the individual and the company benefit when somebody learns something new.

Spend time and money developing the communication and leadership skills of employees as well as their technical skills. Although staying current with rapidly changing technology is important, developing communications and leadership skills of your employees is just as critical. This is especially true if most employees work directly with customers, partners, or suppliers. Employees' ability to communicate ideas and solutions is a critical success factor for every business. Consider a customized client-handling and effective communications program, and if necessary, engage outside experts.

Levels of Initiative

Stephen Covey identified six levels of initiative in his book *Principle-Centered Leadership*.[2] You will be able to trace the growth of employees as they move through Covey's levels:

1. Waiting to be told

2. Asking what to do

3. Recommending solutions

4. Acting and reporting immediately

5. Acting and reporting occasionally

6. Acting on his or her own

In other words, low initiative is characterized by sitting around waiting to be told what to do. High initiative is acting on your own. Employees naturally move through this progression as their skills grow and as they are challenged to exercise higher levels of initiative. A strong, empowered culture will also motivate them to progress more quickly through the stages of initiative.

In an Internal Franchise, the hierarchy extends one additional level. As the five entrepreneurial beliefs permeate your organization, and as engaged entrepreneurial employees begin to execute the operating model, the seventh level of initiative becomes acting as a steward of the business and, in some cases, acting like the owner of the business. At this level, not only do employees act on their own, but they act in ways that will further the vision of the business. Their actions center on executing and improving the operating model. They are ready to internally franchise the operating model and take ownership of their part of the business.

Accountability

History books are filled with stories of great leaders who held themselves accountable to the principles and values in which they believed. The story of George Washington and the cherry tree instilled in school-aged children the belief that you should never tell a lie. Patrick Henry's cry of "Give me liberty or give me death" not only inspired a young republic but reminds all Americans that freedom and liberty are more important than life itself. Martin Luther King's dream of equality and nonviolence inspired a generation of Americans to take action and then stand tall in the face of adversity.

Today, our society has discounted the virtue of accountability. Newspapers constantly run stories about professional athletes and celebrities who violate the law and then dismiss their boorish behavior, blaming their misfortunes on everyone but themselves. Politicians engage in unethical campaigns, illegal fund-raising, and other sordid affairs and then point fingers at the system and the accuser rather than accepting full responsibility. Corporate executives attempt to distance themselves from company wrongdoings while getting rich on compensation packages that have no correlation to corporate performance.

Where have all the George Washingtons, Patrick Henrys, and Martin Luther Kings gone? Why is it that few people seem to hold themselves accountable for their actions? Why don't we ever read about a CEO who forfeited his annual bonus because the company missed its numbers? I'll let the sociologists and pundits debate this, but my experience has shown that given the opportunity, most people do hold themselves accountable for their actions. It's just not considered newsworthy. What's newsworthy is CEOs of Fortune 100 companies receiving compensation packages that are out of line with their companies' long-term growth and profitability.

Petty Politics

One of the ugly yet easily recognizable attributes of an organization that lacks accountability is petty politics. Each person spends a great deal of energy engaged in "watch your back" tactics. This begins to put the emphasis on blame rather than on results. Employees assess the level of blame associated with any failure and then pass it around like a hot potato until someone else gets stuck with it.

For example, almost twenty years ago, one of the business units in our professional service company, which we called accountability centers, won a project to develop a software system for the Internal Revenue Service. Our firm was responsible for developing the software for a system that would match W-2 information with corporate tax returns.

Early in the project, we decided to switch hardware platforms. As a result, we needed to purchase the hardware for the project. Since the IRS delayed ordering the hardware, it was unavailable when we needed it. During one of our status meetings with a number of IRS officials, we discussed the status of the new hardware. Although the software was being written for the IRS's Albany, New York, facility, the Washington headquarters funded it, and John, the person whose job it was to order the hardware, was located there. Although a rather pleasant fellow, he seemed a bit detached from the entire conversation.

When a senior IRS official asked why the hardware wasn't yet ordered, a deafening silence filled the room. Moments later the senior IRS official asked the question, "Aren't you accountable for this, John?" After another long pause, John finally gathered together himself and said, "What do you mean when you say 'accountable'?"

On the flip side, consider the culture of accountability established by Bruce Ballengee of Pariveda Solutions. Ballengee and Pariveda have institutionalized a corporate pillar called the expectations framework where they explicitly state what is expected of everyone in the organization, leaving virtually no room to avoid being accountable.[3]

Many organizations don't even know what the word "accountability" means, much less practice the behaviors associated with accountability. Excuses become the norm in these companies. Finger-pointing is a way to keep oneself out of the reach of the headhunting management group. Recreational complaining replaces positive communication. Being accountable for anything is the farthest thing from these employees' minds.

A strong, empowered culture filled with engaged entrepreneurial employees creates and reinforces accountability. Employees not only hold themselves accountable but also begin to hold others accountable. One of the great powers of this strong culture filled with employees actively executing the operating model is in the fact that blame and judgment are no longer driving forces in the culture. Performance becomes the measure, and it is in everyone's best interest that performance continually

To see if your organization could use an accountability boost, take this test. Are the following statements true about your organization?

- Many people think their career development plans are their responsibility and not their supervisor's.
- Most people have a little too much on their plate.
- Employees are comfortable going outside their own project boundaries or job descriptions in order to get the job done right.
- We take action and follow up on the results of assignments made during meetings.
- We are usually given increased authority, resources, and encouragement when given increased responsibility.
- The leadership takes ownership for the shortcomings as well as the successes of the organization.
- The "way things are" (people, processes, and structure) rarely gets in the way of real progress.
- We know our principles and values and enforce them at all levels.
- We don't engage in finger-pointing or the "blame game" when problems arise.
- When mistakes or failures occur, we think of them as tuition and teach everyone else what we learned.
- Most of our compensation and reward systems reinforce the desired behaviors we need to be successful.

The more times you answered yes, the more accountable your organization is. Too many no answers should make you flinch!

improves. Assessment and improvement replace blame and judgment. The organization as a whole learns and advances.

Companies with high accountability are committed to improvement. They either have established self-improvement processes or have developed an open forum for employees to test theories on improved performance. The improvements became institutionalized and part of the corporate fabric.

Turn Up the Accountability, Please

Some companies just seem to have accountability. Did their employees swallow some sort of accountability pill when they were hired? What are these companies doing to create the environment where all employees take ownership of their actions?

Beyond creating the environment of TRUST discussed earlier, the leadership can take four specific actions to help create additional accountability within your company:

- *Overuse the word "accountability."* Include it in all of your meetings. Define it as it applies to your company. Discuss accountability in your corporate newsletter. Refer to people as being accountable for their areas of responsibility. "Accountability" is a very powerful word, and the more employees begin to use it, the more they will understand its meaning. Create an accountability award. One company, Tenacity Solutions from Reston, Virginia, gives out an employee-driven quarterly "Cat in the Hat" award that stresses results, collaboration, and accountability.

- *Rename your business units "accountability centers."* This is especially important if a business unit is a profit and loss center. The leader in charge of the accountability center is now accountable for everything that goes on in that area. This eliminates the question, "What do you mean when you say accountable?"

- *Develop a meeting model that assigns action items and hold people responsible for completing those items.* How many meetings have you attended where action items were listed and then events seemed to overwhelm the issue and nothing got done? Assign a scribe and keep the notes taken on your company portal. When an action is completed, update the notes and notify the participants. If the action is not completed, the entire team will have a record of the accountable person.

- *Review your current job descriptions.* Job or position descriptions naturally tend to establish parameters outside of which things won't get done. They can institutionalize the dreaded phrase "It's not my job." Rework descriptions to describe roles and corporate objectives rather than putting an overemphasis on specific tasks. Everyone in the company is responsible for making the company successful.

Are Initiative and Accountability Enough?

It would seem that a company that has created a culture where employees show a great deal of initiative and hold themselves accountable for their actions is well on its way to success. This is partly true, but these organizations can still be more successful by understanding that even a high-initiative, high-accountability culture leaves a few holes unfilled. Let's take a look at a matrix that has initiative on the X axis and accountability on the Y axis.

Initiative–Accountability Matrix

High	□ The focus is on systems □ Projects are overmanaged □ People are overcontrolled □ Parochial management is the norm □ Cost cutting is a priority	□ Workers are highly accountable □ Initiatives are completed □ Leaders adapt to change □ Employees look for opportunities □ Responsibilities are embraced
ACCOUNTABILITY	III	IV
	I	II
Low	□ Historical market share is relied upon □ Customers are loyal to a brand □ Innovation is lacking □ Status quo is valued	□ New ideas are the norm □ New projects go unfinished □ Business areas become autonomous □ Compensation rewards high flyers □ Corporate goals take a backseat
	Low	**INITIATIVE** High

Quadrant I

Companies with low initiative and low accountability (quadrant I) simply exist. You can find them grouped in a mature market or even in an institutional setting like academia or government. Sometimes they are large Fortune 500 companies whose time as major players in their industry has come and gone, but they stay alive through strong channels of distribution, customer loyalty to a specific brand, or an overwhelming market share.

Employees in these organizations tend to think of work as a means to a paycheck. The fear of disrupting operations that have worked for fifty years is so strong, employees simply begin to punch the clock, keep their heads down, and pick up their paychecks every two weeks.

Quadrant II

Companies that exhibit high initiative but low accountability (quadrant II) radiate with energy and new ideas, but many projects go unfinished. They are characterized by fits and starts. A company going through an aggressive growth period, perhaps hiring a large sales force and then struggling to meet the new demand, is an example. Employees begin to operate as lone rangers. They are very independent and don't see the need to work together. Compensation systems reward individual performance but are generally not tied to corporate objectives.

During the late 1990s, a group of new Internet-based companies, commonly referred to as dot-coms, experienced this high-initiative, low-accountability mode that is typical of quadrant II. Many of these companies were initially successful, but the lack of accountability became a challenge. One of the high rollers of the dot-com era was *WorldCom*. It was found to be using *illegal accounting practices* to amplify profits on a yearly basis. One argument is the company's leaders were simply crooks, but the more likely argument is the company's governance (accountability) was inadequate and cutting corners became increasingly easy. WorldCom's stock price fell drastically when the information about its accounting became public and eventually the company filed the *third largest corporate bankruptcy in U.S. history.*

Quadrant III

Perhaps the majority of mature companies exist with low initiative and high accountability (quadrant III). In these environments, the focus is on systems. Work and people tend to be overmanaged and overcontrolled. Managers become very parochial and concerned about their territories. They spend energy on bottom-line management instead of top-line revenue creation. They look for ways to cut costs in order to give the impression that productivity and profitability are on the rise.

These companies often have secret mechanisms that circumvent laborious processes that don't actually serve any specific purpose. For example, perhaps a company has a process for expense-account approval, but everybody knows you go to Mary in finance, and she fast-tracks your expense-account approval for you. When I was at Boeing, the employees had large three-ring binders containing many rules collectively called "Policies and Procedures," informally known as "Pols and Pros." These rules were routinely ignored. We would check boxes on forms to indicate that we had followed the Pols and Pros, but we never did. Instead, we took a real-world approach—one that didn't necessarily match up with the approach the procedures and policies required.

This problem is epidemic in second-stage growth businesses. As they continue to grow, second-stage growth businesses begin focusing on their Bottom Line Managers rather than Top Line Leaders. What are bottom-line managers? These managers concentrate on the expense side of the income statement. They sit at their desks with their operating budgets in hand, dutifully reviewing each and every expense to make sure it is in the budget. Organizations can spend thousands of hours developing, reviewing, and reconciling operational budgets and very little time discussing their customers.

Top-line leaders, on the other hand, focus on the revenue side of the equation. They understand that the only way to create new opportunities is to find new customers. Top-line leaders focus on substantially increasing revenues by finding new niches, developing new or modified products and services, or expanding geographically or online. Top-line leaders build a leadership team that includes bottom-line managers, but the top-line leader is always first among equals.

Many growing companies experience an overwhelming urge to put in place a manager who begins to control expenses. Obviously, expense control is important and essential to a company's long-term health, but revenue generation and the expansion of the top line should drive expense decisions. Stagnant businesses have an abundance of bottom-line managers, but what they need is top-line leadership.

Entrepreneurial companies must focus on revenue generation first and expense control second. Reward systems must reinforce the idea that profit results from revenue creation, not from simply slashing costs.

Quadrant IV

Companies that create a trusting environment will create a culture of high initiative and high accountability (quadrant IV). High initiative creates opportunities that are completed by highly accountable people. The organization continues to grow, leaders continue to innovate and make adaptive changes, and employees continue to seek out responsibility. It's almost utopia!

A company needs to look for a couple of additional signs of growth, signs that indicate the company is marshalling resources from all over the organization to meet customer needs. These signs mark the elimination of parochial and territorial thinking, indicating that initiative and accountability are focused in the right direction. These are signs that high-performing teams and external focus are present.

The creation of a high-initiative, high-accountability workforce is essential as a company moves toward a strong, empowered workplace. Over time, initiative and accountability become localized and the company finds ways for those units to become interdependent. Companies consisting of high-initiative, high-accountability business units still will not reach their potential unless these units begin to rely on each other as a force multiplier.

High-Performing Teams

That's where high-performing teams come into play. First, individuals show signs of exercising initiative and accepting accountability. As those individuals interact with other members of the organization, they form work groups. As the work groups become more sophisticated and need to share ideas and solutions, they form teams. These teams take on a life of their own.

Companies without high-performing teams are filled with employees who don't understand how the vision of the organization relates to them. The success of their individual actions determines their motivations. They don't consider corporate or business unit objectives as they make business decisions throughout the day. The workforce doesn't know the vision and mission of the organization, so they have little motivation to align their actions with the vision.

Employees can more easily meet corporate objectives when they know what those objectives are, why they are important to reach, and what the positive and negative consequences are for reaching or not reaching those objectives. Companies with low-performing teams often have a nonaligned reward system.

When leaders leave team goals out of the equation, employees remain independent. However, the real objective is helping them reach a state of interdependence.

The Help Model

The Help Model is an effective tool for developing team spirit. Use the Help Model as a force multiplier to expand your ability to service customers. The Help Model can be thought of as a win-win-win arrangement. The company wins because expertise is leveraged and holes are plugged in service and product offerings, employees win because they have the opportunity to expand their personal competencies, and customers win because the whole of the organization serving them is indeed greater than the sum of its parts.

Use the Help Model as a force multiplier to expand your ability to service customers.

The Help Model can keep today's little problem from becoming tomorrow's major corporate challenge. As problems begin to manifest themselves and affect individual or business unit performance, seeking help becomes critical in the development of any organization. Not asking for help leaves you with a very high probability of repeating the mistakes of the past. Asking for and receiving help allows you to minimize the consequences of a bad situation and can provide a solution to the problem.

Companies that have cracked the code to cooperation have a tremendous advantage. They go to market armed with the courage, competency, and intellectual capital of an entire workforce. Individuals can attack the most difficult problem, call the most difficult client, and stretch their comfort zones with the full faith that their organization stands ready to assist them should a situation begin to go wrong.

The ability to work as a team can become a huge competitive advantage. Consider service firms that typically engage the customer with individuals or small teams of two or three. For example, cable television technicians, plumbers, and heating and air conditioning repairpersons are armed with the knowledge that they are supported by a knowledgeable and service-oriented workforce.

Company leaders must encourage employees to rely on one another. Teach them to seek help if they don't know the answer to a question or have the part or product they need. If they are stuck on a technical issue, instruct them to find an expert in the company and bring that expert to the customer's site to fix the problem.

This process must become an integral part of your operating model. Systems have to be built to support the customer. For example, our home recently experienced a poor cable television picture. A Comcast technician diagnosed the problem and informed me that I would need to have the signal amplified. The problem was, he was out of amplifiers on his truck so I would have to wait until the next day. But one short call to the service center located another technician just down the street with a number of extra amplifiers, my technician ran down the street, picked up the amplifier; and made a quick installation and a happy customer all in one fell swoop. The system supported an empowered employee trying his best to win over a customer!

The help model leverages the expertise of the entire organization and provides a force multiplier to every employee who participates. Companies that still live in a parochial stovepipe world are doomed to rely on individual skills for their success, while companies that embrace the help model build an enriched workforce with employees willing to tackle almost any challenge. Sure, you'll have superstars and heroes in your ranks, but the best leaders know real riches lie only in a supportive cast.

Beware of the Heroes

Many companies get caught in the trap of relying on heroes. So many companies in challenging economic times have flattened out. They've had some success in the past, but they are now facing a flat top line or, worse, their top line is shrinking. Sometimes this is the result of the "hero paradigm," where companies succeed based on the activities of a hero or a set of heroes. These companies eventually flatten out because they lack process, structure, and methodology (the bane of entrepreneurs), and they can't scale.

A quick litmus test for your company to see if your success is dependent on heroes is to listen carefully to your language of success. How do you describe success?

For example, some leaders will talk about opening up a new market with a comment like, "We were successful in the Southwest because of John's contacts and his ability to push through sales during the last quarter." Can you imagine Eric Schmidt of Google or Larry Ellison of Oracle saying, "We attribute our success in India to the ability of Mary Jane and her knowledge of corporate IT buying behavior!"

While some companies rely on heroes to be successful, others learn to scale, and although they certainly have superstars on their teams, they've learned how to repeat their successes by leveraging individual competencies, not relying on them.

Most companies have yet to figure out that asking for help is not a sign of weakness. It is actually a sign of intelligence. Problem solving is rarely best performed in a vacuum. It works best with input from a variety of sources. Those with experience must share it. Those with fresh ideas must be heard. And even those who say something can't be done have a voice (but only a small voice!). The ultimate responsibility for the decision is not abdicated. It still lies in the hands of the person asking for help, but that person should feel compelled to search for other opinions.

Let's look at the Help Model in more detail. It consists of the following steps:

- Anticipate the need.

- Ask for help.

- Become a servant leader.

- Show appreciation.

Anticipate the Need

The first step in asking for help is anticipating the need. Make every attempt to understand your situation and anticipate your needs. Seek help before issues turn into a bubbling caldron. Allow time for a response from those willing to help. Determine that what you are about to ask help for is important and not just urgent. Think about the unfortunate shepherd boy of bedtime fame. You will be able to cry wolf only so many times before everyone will ignore you.

Ask for Help

Seeking out help doesn't make you less of a technician or a manager. It makes you better! Think of the alternatives. You can select one of the most feasible options with the hope that it will be the right choice, or you can call your counterpart in another business unit that you know has faced a similar problem before.

The choice seems clear, yet in many corporate cultures, asking for help is viewed as a weakness. This prehistoric position is most likely a holdover from a period in our industrial development when situations just didn't change much. If a manager didn't know the production capability of a sheet-metal extrusion furnace, he was considered incompetent—and perhaps rightfully so. However, times have changed. Everyone's job is more complicated today. More people are responsible for complete business processes rather than just tasks. And business processes are multidisciplinary. In this environment, is it fair to consider employees incompetent if they ask for help? The answer is no.

As a leader in one of today's rapidly changing companies, you must create an environment that is conducive to asking for help. Your employees don't have all the answers. The most experienced managers don't have all the answers. No one person does, but in an organization embracing the Help Model, the opportunity for coming up with the right answer will increase dramatically.

All employees must always feel they can ask for help. They can seek help using communications tools such as e-mail, voice mail, Web conferencing, texting, wikis, social networking, the corporate portal, as well as just about any tool the Web has to offer.

When asking for help, people should use the following tips. Be clear and concise. State exactly what you want. Make it as easy as possible for someone to help you. Explain the significance of the question you are trying to answer and how the outcome will affect the project or corporate goals. Finally, if the request is for significant time, be prepared to build a short business case to support your request. Asking a quick question regarding the air-travel system in Morocco is on a different scale than asking someone to travel there for a site inspection. Anticipate the scale of your need and be explicit in your request.

Become a Servant Leader

As the Help Model begins to work, your entire organization will become sensitive to the concept that asking for help is not a sign of weakness; it is a strength encouraged by management. This leads to a quick realization that if the company encourages asking for help, then it must also encourage providing help.

An underlying theme in the successful implementation of an Internal Franchise is becoming a servant leader. Robert Greenleaf, the deceased founder of the Robert K. Greenleaf Center for Servant Leadership and perhaps the world's best-known writer on the topic of servant leadership, felt that true leadership emerges from those whose primary motivation is a desire to help others. For the Help Model to be effective in any corporate culture, there must be evidence that this motivation exists.

Becoming a servant leader means that you make serving others—employees, customers, and the community—your top priority. In the Help Model, the servant leader is sensitive to the needs of others. Begin by putting yourself in their shoes. Make every effort to understand the need and what is being asked.

Servant leaders listen, have empathy, and then try to improve the person's situation. At times this means responding immediately with an answer. Other times it means pointing someone in the right direction. Sometimes persuasion will be your most effective tool. Use every method of communication available with the goal of providing immediate relief and eventual insight.

As the organization creates an awareness of the importance of serving, you'll sense the development of community. Division walls will seem less impenetrable. Organizational boundaries will not keep people from serving and helping others in the organization. The sales group will understand the issues facing manufacturing. Marketing will understand that it can't promote products that are not available yet. In short, employees will begin to look at issues not just from their own point of view; they will have an interest in serving the needs of others for the good of the entire organization.

Show Appreciation

Consider Maria, running through the halls looking for help for an urgent problem. When help comes her way, she is quick to accept it but slow to acknowledge it. Two weeks later, she pokes her head in every door, looking for someone to solve the same problem. Not only will the outstretched arms of a fortnight ago turn into crossed arms, Maria will have begun to develop the reputation as one who uses the Help Model for the wrong reasons.

Not only was she unappreciative, she took no steps to fortify her personal competencies by learning from her first experience with the Help Model.

The Help Model has three communication components. First, you ask for help. Then a colleague meets your needs. Finally, and perhaps most importantly, you acknowledge the help and grow from the experience. Failing in this final step will make the tool more difficult to use in the future. Not acknowledging the help will make you seem unappreciative. Failing to document the help and learn from your experience will cause your colleagues to view you as lazy and incompetent.

When you show appreciation, make it public. A brief e-mail, a voice mail, a Tweet, or a handwritten note thanking the person whose help you received goes a long way in perpetuating the model. A handshake in private sends a strong message. A handshake in the presence of the helping person's supervisor supports and encourages an environment where serving others remains a priority.

As you show appreciation, realize that you needed help because you were weak in some area of expertise. Resolve to mitigate that weakness as part of your personal development plan.

The Help Model can have a profound impact on an organization. The real strength of growing companies lies in their ability to create synergies between individuals within the business. Cooperative synergies leverage the skills and abilities from one unit with a weakness to another unit with a strength. The Help Model serves as the conduit for this type of synergy.

External Focus

You've created a culture of high initiative and high accountability. Disparate business units have begun to create synergies throughout the organization using the Help Model. Now it's time to make sure your organization remains focused on the right target. An organization that shows the first three signs of growth will still not be productive if it directs its energy inward. It must focus externally. Companies rarely go out of business because their internal processes are a mess. They go out of business when customers stop buying their products and services. If you stay focused on your customers, you will eventually get a chance to fix your poorly functioning processes. The reverse is not always true. It may be too late to fix anything internally if you've neglected your customer base.

Is it important for even the support elements of your business, such as accounting and human resources, to have an external focus? Yes. Developing an external focus throughout the organization is a way to live your vision. How many times have you read a mission or vision statement that said, "We endeavor to have the best inventory control process by the year 2015"? The answer is never. Your mission is about your customers. Therefore, everyone in your organization must be focused on customers.

Companies with an external focus target new ventures, look for new markets, and expand their services to current customers. Companies with an internal focus build facilities to support the hierarchy within the company. Externally focused companies concentrate on increasing revenues. Internally focused companies concentrate on cutting costs. The more externally focused an organization is, the more in tune it is with the customer and market. Externally focused companies have built-in customer-focused teams. They know the market trends because they live in the market. They understand the needs of their customers because they spend a great deal of time with them.

Conclusion

When your Internal Franchise takes root, you will see your employees exercising initiative to create value for your customers and profit for your business. They will accept accountability for their actions. They will support each other and leverage your organization's total capabilities when serving customers. And they will remain focused on the customers, not internal politics. The first signs that your Internal Franchise is working are initiative, accountability, high-performing teams, and an external focus. It's critical that you have all four present in your organization.

Initiative without accountability results in a lot of activity but not a lot of responsibility. People may act, but they aren't going to take responsibility for their actions. When initiative and accountability work together, people act and accept responsibility, but they act alone. They have a narrow, parochial view of their roles.

When initiative, accountability, and high-performing teams work together, progress begins to be made. Your entire organization works together as a team. People act, take responsibility for their actions, and help others become successful as well. They understand that the success of the company is most important. They understand that what's good for the franchise system is good for the franchisee.

Finally, when you add external focus to the mix, you have an explosive formula for business success. Now, your employee team is focused on serving the customers together! They accept accountability for making customers happy. They work together to identify new opportunities. They stay focused on the future and your vision for the business. Their goal is to be the best that they can be together. Your Internal Franchise has begun to sprout!

Now what? What happens next? Like any good farmer, when your seedlings sprout, you weed and feed. You nurture the small plants so they remain healthy and produce an abundant harvest. In an Internal Franchise, weeding and feeding means leadership. And that's the subject of our next chapter.

8

Leading the Internal Franchise

WHY DO WE need leadership? Why do we need a management team? What value do they provide the organization? The truth is we would really have no need for management or anyone in a leadership position if we could only be assured there would be no more change. Change is a constant, however, so every organization needs strong leadership to create a vision or establish a direction and then align the organization with that direction. Organizations that can develop leaders prepared to deal with and lead change will prosper. Those that don't will rise and fall with market trends and eventually fade away.

In an Internal Franchise, the need for leadership does not begin and end in the executive suite. In fact, if you have an executive suite, you may want to get rid of it! As I interviewed senior executives in a variety of industries for this book, only a few times did I have to press a special elevator button or be escorted to the executive wing of the building. Obviously the business community is making progress in this area.

Leadership should not be a quality attributed to only a few individuals at the top of an organization. Change becomes much easier and more effective when the ability to make sound business decisions is distributed throughout the organization. Teaching everyone in the company about the organization is very useful; when everyone knows how the business works, all employees understand their role in its success and how their work is integral to that success. Leadership, then, becomes ubiquitous throughout the organization. If even junior managers know how everything affects the bottom line it will be easier for them to make business decisions that are more productive and cost-effective. This form of transparency can be a huge benefit for the organization, especially when it seeks to change a deep-seated way of doing business.

The need for leadership permeates every organization. Presidents and CEOs clearly must be effective leaders, but so must each project leader. The CFO must align his team with the financial goals of the organization, but he also must translate those financial goals into tangible actions so the operational staff can get excited about them. Business unit managers must translate the corporate vision into realistic and attainable goals. Sales directors need to set examples of professionalism and customer focus. Supervisors must recognize great performance and celebrate accomplishments.

The Law of the Harvest for an Internal Franchise suggests that each time you begin to see signs of growth, signs that the Internal Franchise is working, then your job as a leader is to nourish these signs. Feed the positive attributes and weed out the barriers and roadblocks to success. Remove anything that gets in the way of increased accountability, increased initiative, increased team spirit, and an increased external focus. And don't just clip off the tops of the weeds. Weeds have a way of reappearing. Dig down for the entire root.

Along with the continuous and often backbreaking job of weeding goes the fun and exciting job of feeding your new seedlings. Remember, you must condition the soil. The fundamental assumption is the seeds are fine, and a combination of nutrient-rich soil and your constant attention will make for a plentiful harvest. Feeding means making sure you have the right conditions for success and minimizing the effects of detrimental conditions.

The Law of the Harvest for an Internal Franchise suggests that each time you begin to see signs of growth, signs that the Internal Franchise is working, then your job as a leader is to nourish these signs.

Your responsibilities as a leader in an Internal Franchise are simple to discuss but quite difficult to execute. The good news for you, however, is that the constant process of weeding and feeding is very natural. It's not based on any Ivy League–created leadership mantra; it's based on the simple Law of the Harvest: you reap what you sow.

Leadership and Change

As we said before, we wouldn't need anyone in a position of leadership if nothing ever changed. We all could just do our jobs and everything would be great. But what if the union demands higher wages? What if the client decided you were too expensive? What if three of your colleagues find new employment and leave you with three times as much work? Someone will have to make a decision, someone will have to look at the implications of that decision, and someone must make sure that the decision balances the interests of all the company stakeholders. That someone is a leader.

When you introduce the concepts of this book into your organization, you will already have made the fundamental decision to alter how business currently is done. Introducing any kind of change takes leadership. Cultural change requires leadership infused with a sound process for implementing change.

Whether you are the president of a business unit or CEO of the entire organization, your ability to fully implement an Internal Franchise throughout the organization will be in direct relationship to your ability to lead change. The task is doable but takes constant attention. Remember, any kind of change that is not initiated and supported by the leader will invariably fail. If you already have some type of positional power, your chances of succeeding increase dramatically. If you are a team leader, regional manager, or business unit leader, your objective must be to create franchises and then constantly communicate the benefits of the business model throughout the organization.

Machiavelli said, "There is nothing more difficult to take in hand, more perilous to conduct, or more uncertain in its success, than to take the lead in the introduction of a new order of things."[1] Smart man that Machiavelli! If you've been in a leadership position for more than five minutes, you know how true this is.

The Mind, Body, and Soul of an Organization

A useful way to think of strategies for effective organizational change is to imagine three rocks held together by a rubber band. The rocks represent the mind, body, and soul of an organization. All three must move forward at the same time or the rubber band will snap back, stymieing progress and leaving you, at best, in the same position as when you started the change initiative.

The "mind" of an organization is its leadership—those making decisions at all levels of an organization. Leaders are the ones who are setting strategy and articulating a vision and direction.

The "body" of an organization consists of the processes, the structure, and even the finances of the organization. The body represents the moving parts of an organization. The "soul" of an organization, informing both the mind and the body, is the corporate culture—what is accepted in an organization, a kind of code of ethics.

Any change strategy has to move all three of these elements in unison (or close to it) if it is to be successful in the long run. The metaphor of the rocks held together by a rubber band is a reminder of the challenges of leading a successful change effort. Every transformational initiative represents change, and since change is the only constant in business, learning to effectively lead the change is the only way to ensure survival.

Moving the Mind

Thomas Jefferson said the "dispositions of the mind, like limbs of the body, acquire strength by exercise."[2] The mind of an organization is its leadership. If we don't exercise our leadership, it will atrophy and become useless. In moving the mind of the organization forward, we first need to perform a critical skills assessment of the leadership. This assessment must be more general and all-encompassing than the kinds of superficial assessments you might have experienced. Some sort of team-based assessment, called a 360-degree assessment, is probably advisable. A 360-degree assessment is an evaluation of leadership capability in general. It addresses all the classic leadership attributes, from establishing direction to aligning processes to motivating and inspiring.

If we don't exercise our leadership, it will atrophy and become useless.

A thorough leadership assessment also assesses classic management skills like controlling, monitoring, and delegating. A 360-degree assessment shows the level of functioning of both a leader and that leader's circle of influence. The leader may very well be good at certain parts of leadership—say, the intellectual/financial side—but lack certain key qualities of emotion or vision. A 360-degree assessment allows for both strengths and weaknesses to be highlighted. Every leader within the organization, from the CEO and supervisors to coworkers and subordinates, goes through this process because the goal for growth is not just for one person to have the skills to move forward but for the entire leadership as a whole to have those skills as a group. The most important part of an organization's growth is the advancement of the mind, though it cannot happen without the simultaneous growth of the other sectors.

Assessment is generally very successful if it is approached enthusiastically by an organization. It can be tied to new planning initiatives and development of weaker skills. And it's important to remember that the identification of strong skills is just as important as the identification of weaknesses. Strengths, after all, will be your leverage points. But the assessment of all these aspects is what's most important and is crucial to preparing for growth.

As we have seen, it is important that leadership not be a quality perceived as residing in only a few individuals at the top of an organization. Executives can promote this ubiquitous leadership by sharing their knowledge with other members of the organization. It can be as simple as telling everyday stories that make it easier to understand how the organization works and how individual employees' work has an impact on an organization.

Craig McIntosh of Acrylon Plastics said that when he first took the leadership reins, individual plant managers "didn't know they were in financial trouble" because critical financial information was simply not shared. So, he implemented a policy of transparency and took advantage of their competitive nature, and over time, each plant moved into the black.[3] Employees at King Arthur Flour, ranked as one of Vermont's Best Places to Work, share their knowledge another way. They participate in monthly town hall meetings. These one-hour meetings are chaired by Steve Voigt, the CEO, but they quickly become wide-open forums for sharing ideas and questioning policies and procedures.[4]

Changing the Body

When considering the body of an organization, remember the image of the three rocks held together by a rubber band. If the three rocks don't move together, they will certainly not be able to move separately. An organization's body is its procedures and structure, the core processes the company needs to work well. These can range from inventory control to sales turnover to professional services delivery. These processes must be looked at critically—just as the organization's leadership is analyzed—to make sure that they can handle the extra pressure of change. Are the organization's structures aligned with the vision for its future? If business transformation and reengineering are necessary to support a change, it is crucial this be determined before the change process begins.

When the processes of an organization are changed, they must be aligned with one another. (In keeping with the image, the little pebbles among the rocks must be held together, just as the big rocks are held to each other.) Structural realignment is not the only thing that is important to change in the body of the organization. The individual elements of the body may be fine, but their alignment may be problematic. In that case, it is important to realign processes appropriately to ensure that they will not be overwhelmed by change.

Expressing the Soul

The underpinning of the mind and body is the soul, the culture of an organization. A culture is the glue of the organization. It holds some areas together when other areas fall apart at the leadership or process level. It represents the company's code of values.

Useful methods and techniques are available for assessing the soul of the organization, and once a code of values is established, it should be publicized. So what are your company values and ideals? Have you laid out a set of ideals that people can share? Are you constantly motivating employees to align themselves behind your shared values? The best ideals pass the test of time. Ideals give meaning to your corporate purpose and answer the question of why you open your doors every day, whether that door is online or on Main Street. Values are your filtering mechanism for helping you make the right decisions.

When considering your ideals, ask yourself the following questions:

- What do you think about most often?

- Where do you spend most of your free time?

- Where do you spend your capital?

- What pleases you most about the direction of your business?

When considering your corporate values, engage your leadership team in an exercise of developing a list of shared values. Start with an exercise introduced by Ken Blanchard in his book *Managing by Values*.[5] I've used this exercise with Fortune 100 executives in a small mahogany-paneled conference room as well as hundreds of teenagers in the Eisenhower Theatre of the Kennedy Center and it never fails to produce amazing results.

As the instructions indicate, start with everyone picking the values that strike an individual chord. Then make each participant narrow that list to three. Then force each person to turn to their neighbor and compromise on a new list of three. Continue the exercise, each time combining groups until you finally have one list of three shared values upon which the

OUR VALUES

The most important thing in life is to decide what is most important.

What should our organization, department, unit, or team stand for? What should be the values by which we operate? Look over the list of values below. Circle any values that "jump out" because of their importance to you. Then, write your *top three* values, in order of importance, below the list. Feel free to add values if needed.

Truth	Sincerity	Dependability
Efficiency	Fun	Trust
Initiative	Relationships	Excellence
Environmentalism	Wisdom	Teamwork
Power	Flexibility	Service
Control	Perspective	Profitability
Competition	Commitment	Freedom
Excitement	Recognition	Friendship
Creativity	Learning	Influence
Happiness	Honesty	Justice
Honor	Originality	Quality
Innovation	Candor	Hard work
Obedience	Prosperity	Responsiveness
Financial growth	Respect	Fulfillment
Community support	Fairness	Purposefulness
Integrity	Order	Strength
Peace	Spirituality	Self-control
Loyalty	Adventure	Cleverness
Clarity	Cooperation	Success
Security	Humor	Stewardship
Love	Collaboration	Support
Persistence	Resources	

1. _____

2. _____

3. _____

entire group can agree. Every organization should post their values. This will help justify tough decisions because such decisions—over hiring and firing, for instance—can be persuasively articulated when they can be connected with the organization's value system.

In most organizations, the code of behavior—concerning issues like lateness and timeliness, dress, and approach to customers—is left largely unspoken. This is a potential problem. Important aspects of the culture must be clear and documented. Make sure that new people are brought into the organization in accordance with this code. It can even be used as a selling point, attesting to an organization's commitment to its customers and employees. Documenting these unspoken codes can be very effective. Keep in mind that for the issues of organizational culture, "If it's not written down, it doesn't exist."

Some organizations have an easier time with this change process than others. If your organization is steeped in traditional management hierarchy and dotted with pockets of parochial, inward-thinking management, then the process will be more difficult to implement. On the other hand, if your organization realizes there is a new employment contract between companies and employees and that in many industries employees can and do find fulfilling employment, then the opportunity for success is very real. Ironically, organizations that most need an Internal Franchise are the ones that have the most difficult time implementing many of its features and recognizing its benefits.

COACH

The mnemonic for teaching people how to lead in an Internal Franchise is COACH. Most of us can easily relate to the concepts of coaching.

- **C**ommunicate at all times.

- **O**versee teams.

- **A**lign the organization with its purpose.

- **C**reate the next generation of leaders.

- Create a **H**igher purpose.

Whether we're watching the T-ball and soccer games of our children or professional football, we know the attributes of a good coach. Good coaches instruct and demonstrate. They have a very good understanding of how the game is played and how best to compete and win. Good coaches have excellent communication skills. They can motivate and inspire players in one-on-one sessions or in large group settings. Good coaches help orchestrate team members' actions and movements. They are intimately familiar with the dynamics of groups and teams and the necessity of working together. Finally, good coaches establish goals for which the teams willingly strive and make sacrifices. They set the bar just high enough to get that little extra out of their teams.

Great coaches don't just roam the sidelines of the National Football League. They also organize smooth-running workplaces. Coaches run our community associations and local charities. They are leaders in families, communities, churches, and even politics. Coaches are not just business leaders; they are leaders in the big game of life.

Communicate

An Internal Franchise has at its core the belief that constant and effective communications will occur throughout the organization. This means communications up, down, and laterally. All people in the organization must believe that effective and constant communication will benefit the organization, will benefit their local work situation, and finally, will benefit them personally. Authenticity is the most important factor of effective communications. Nick Morgan, the author of *Trust Me: Four Steps to Authenticity and Charisma*, has spent a lifetime teaching people to be more authentic in their communications. He recommends considering the following goals in your communications. Although Nick devised these techniques for formal presentations, they can be effectively used in virtually any setting.[6]

- *Be open to your audience.* Practice your speech or motivational talk by envisioning what it would be like to give your presentation to someone with whom you're completely comfortable. This is the emotional state you want to be in when you deliver the speech.

- *Connect with your audience.* Did anyone nod off the last time you spoke to a group? Leaders must develop techniques to draw in attendees that may have slipped away. Imagine a bubble around you and your audience. Try to feel the emotions in the bubble. Connect with your audience by considering their current emotional state. Learning a few techniques that can help you connect with your audience will make the presentation more meaningful to you and your audience.

- *Be passionate about your topic.* Ask yourself what aspect of the topic you feel deeply about. What's at stake? What results do you want your presentation or conversation to produce? Focus not on what you want to say but on why you're speaking and how you feel about it. (I once listened to a speech by a CTO who said the difference between his firm and all the other tech firms in the market was the passion with which his firm delivered its services—and he said it with passion! I was convinced!)

- *"Listen" to your audience.* This may be the toughest goal to fulfill. When you step up to begin your presentation, think about what your listeners are likely feeling. Are they excited about the future? Worried about bad news? Upset that they've been forced to attend your meeting? As you practice, imagine watching them closely, looking for signs of their response to you.

Great leaders constantly communicate about the customer, the company, and the future. Make good use of any time you spend with colleagues and subordinates. Think outside the box and challenge employees on what benefits customers see from doing business with your company. Constantly reinforce the vision and direction of the organization by citing examples you see every day.

If colleagues on your staff remain focused on small, tactical issues, ensure that you communicate the big picture to them. If they reject more responsibility and authority, make sure you communicate how the company works. If people are stuck in the status quo, communicate the possibilities for the future.

Share Your Knowledge

Now, let's talk about the content of your message. In virtually every organization, the communication of shared knowledge is critical to profitable operations. In its simplest form, shared knowledge is simply the leveraging of work you've done in the past. We all leverage knowledge in our own way by learning from our mistakes. We become knowledgeable through our readings and experiences. When we pass those experiences on to others, we are sharing our knowledge.

For example, if you've ever made the mistake of putting dishwashing liquid into a dishwashing machine, you quickly experience a kitchen floor full of bubbles. Sharing that somewhat embarrassing knowledge with family and friends will keep others from doing the same—hopefully.

The same should be true in business. When you solve a specific client problem after months of effort, the feeling of individual satisfaction can be like winning your own little World Cup. You feel like you're on top of the world. However, if the knowledge gained through that trial-and-error period is never shared throughout the organization, the same mistake will undoubtedly be repeated. Past corporate experience won't be leveraged because the leadership did not encourage it and no communication tools were in place to facilitate the knowledge transfer.

So not only do you need to be motivated to communicate corporate achievement, you also need to have the tools to make sure you are effectively communicating. Sharing knowledge is just a way to transfer or share institutional lessons learned across organizational boundaries. To share knowledge, the organization has to capture, organize, and find ways to distribute this knowledge to employees that may benefit from its availability. Some consulting firms specialize in helping companies share knowledge, and associations and magazines promote best practices, but the important concept for our purpose is that leadership promotes and the culture supports the ability to share knowledge freely.

The Courage to Communicate

"Courage" is not a word we often bandy about in conference rooms and cubicles. *Webster's* defines courage as "the mental or moral strength to venture, persevere, and withstand danger, fear, or difficulty."[7] But taken in the context of business leadership, courage can also be defined as the ability to talk to employees about what matters to them—and to tell it like it is.

Facing economic challenges or shifting market conditions can be a drain for most leaders. But consider the emotional toll on the workforce. The leaders hold most of the cards. They generally have a feel for the challenges ahead and certainly understand their current financial position. Employees, on the other hand, are generally left wondering, "Is the company doing well?" "Will there be layoffs or other cost-cutting measures?"

This is when courageous leaders really shine. Courage dictates that you tell the whole truth. Holding open, honest, and transparent conversations on current market conditions and the need for change separates the weak leader from the courageous one. Being courageous also means having the confidence to talk not only about the challenges but also about the need for action in order to change direction. Courageous leaders face the facts, clearly describe the plan to meet the pressing challenges, and then reengage employees to become part of the solutions.

Employees don't expect you to be the next "Great Communicator"; however, you will be expected to determine a message (your business purpose and operating model) and then stay on that message. Remember, you should go home every night having fulfilled this statement: "If you're not sick of communicating, you probably haven't done it enough."

Oversee Team Progress

The next item in our COACH mnemonic is to oversee team progress.

In chapter 7, we discussed the development of high-performing teams as a sign of growth in an Internal Franchise. If an Internal Franchise is to be truly effective, the workplace must move through the evolution of individual accomplishments, to group achievements, to reaching team goals, and finally, to becoming a turbocharged team.

The team leadership model for an Internal Franchise centers on Ken Blanchard's Situational Leadership.[8] In a nutshell, Blanchard suggests that all teams evolve through four stages. First, in the orientation stage, everyone is a little confused, usually excited, unsure what to do next. The second stage is dissatisfaction, when the team realizes the volume of the workload and the unrealistic expectations placed upon them. Resolution is the third stage, as the team bears down and makes the best of their schedule, resources, and conditions. Finally, in the fourth stage, production, the team clicks and makes progress.

Now, just because there are four sequential stages doesn't mean your team can't zoom through one stage or fall back a stage or two. As in any real-life project, your team is constrained by schedules, goals, and resources, as well as individual competencies and personalities. Situational Leadership only provides a framework for guiding your actions as your team evolves.

As a leader in an Internal Franchise, your style will change according to the situation in which you find yourself. The Situational Leadership model works extremely well in most environments but especially in project-oriented work environments. Make sure you help your team constantly renew their belief in the purpose of the organization and their belief in the operating model. Better business decisions will result, and people will be secure in the knowledge they are working toward targets as part of a bigger picture.

As a leader in stage one, orientation, you'll be more directive. You'll develop skills, clarify roles, and establish ground rules. In stage two, as dissatisfaction sets in, you should think of coaching people more than directing them. You'll sharpen your conflict resolution skills as team members struggle to find their place on the team.

During stage three, resolution, your leadership style will become more supportive as you see signs of franchise growth appear. When you notice an increase in initiative, accountability, team spirit, and external focus, you should reward that behavior in a public way. The entire team will resolve that this is the way the team is going to work, and you'll notice even more signs of growth.

Finally, in the production stage, you'll need to delegate completely. You'll encourage the team members to act on their own, to act like owners. Your role as a leader will be to monitor goals and performance and keep your hands off a good situation. It is in this stage that many young leaders—and especially young entrepreneurs—begin to meddle. They practice "seagull management": they can hardly believe the project is going well so they swoop in and foul things up!

Situational Leadership works great as a model for leading teams in an Internal Franchise. Recognize the stage you're in and align your leadership style and techniques with that stage. The days of having one way to lead are over. You can't always change your team to fit your style of leadership. Most times you must play the hand you are dealt.

Align the Organization with Its Purpose

We've covered communications and overseeing team progress from the COACH mnemonic; now, we move to aligning the organization with its purpose.

Have you ever driven a car that was badly in need of a front-end alignment? The car drifts in one direction and whenever you take your hands off the wheel, you're headed for the ditch. This car is a great example of how a company functions when its business constructs and workforce are not aligned with the overall purpose of the organization. The company gradually becomes harder and harder to steer until one day it ends up in a ditch.

An Empowering Organizational Structure

One dimension of a business that directly affects alignment is the organization's structure. Small companies naturally avoid hierarchical management structures because the cost of several layers of management is prohibitive. More established companies develop layers for the purpose of oversight and governance. Organizations that have few layers of management are known as flat organizations. Often, flat organizations are synonymous with empowered organizations. The reason is simple.

If there are no managers to make the decisions, the people doing the work of the organization make the decisions. It's empowerment out of necessity. The challenge is to maintain empowerment as the organization grows and the need for management increases.

The traditional, hierarchical organization structure worked well in the past but increasingly has lost its reason for being. Where once hierarchical structures were used to aid communication throughout the organization, today's communication tools can do the job instead. And as most organizations now know, middle management adds to overhead costs while reducing the ability of the organization to adapt to customer needs. When the decision-making process of the organization is fragmented because of hierarchy, it will never be as flexible as an organization that empowers the people closest to the customer.

As an organization grows, the need to manage its size and scope requires additional policies, procedures, processes, governance, and structure. How does the organization balance empowerment and hierarchy? What is the most effective organization structure for an empowered organization?

The goal of any organizational structure should be to push authority and accountability down to the people who serve the customer. That is where decisions must be made. The purpose of the organizational structure is similar to the role of business processes and systems that we discussed earlier. The organizational structure establishes roles that focus on increasing empowerment.

Management roles in the modern organization are communication roles. Think of managers as signposts throughout the organization. They are like the highway information signs that tell us the location of the nearest gas station, restaurant, or hotel. When empowered employees need resources, guidance, or help, managers can point them in the right direction. This means that managers are not responsible for supervising people; instead, they must constantly stay on top of what is going on across the organization. This is in contrast to the traditional view that managers focus only on their slice of the business: their project, business unit, or department. Today, managers need to focus broadly across the organization. They need to know where the resources are and how best to allocate them. Then they must relay this information to the people closest to the customer. When someone has an issue or a need, the manager's job is to point him in the right direction and to marshal the resources needed.

Avoid a semantic battle over the definition of a flat organization. The real issues are whether employees are empowered and whether the organization's structure is aligned to the purpose of the company. The number of managers or management layers is inconsequential. Many organizations have removed middle management layers through layoffs. But a big difference exists between a flat, empowered organization and one gutted by reengineering and downsizing.

To determine whether you have a flat and empowered organization, always look at the fundamental conditions of empowerment and alignment. If your employees can go home at night, look in the mirror, and honestly believe they are empowered to act, have the information and knowledge to act appropriately, and have the unconditional support of the organization behind them, you have an empowered organization. When you have the sense that you live and die by the actions and decisions of your employees, you have an empowered organization. After that, the number of management layers is unimportant. Focus on building the structure, processes, and systems that encourage and support empowerment and are aligned with the purpose of the company.

No matter how empowered an organization you think you run, it places constraints on employees. Of course, not all constraints are bad. In fact, an organization with no constraints can be a little dangerous—exciting, but still dangerous. The kind of constraints that are problems are those that keep employees "inside the box." Some of these are cultural; some are in the form of standard operating procedures; still others are constraints that leaders consider simply habits. As a leader, you must strive to break down all the constraints, old habits, and outdated processes that may divert you from your objectives. But know that any alignment that doesn't recognize the real significance of workplace constraints is positioned for failure.

Leaders in an Internal Franchise focus on aligning both the business constructs and the workforce with the overall purpose of the organization. The business constructs are the systems, policies, and procedures that serve as the backbone of the organization. They help us get paid and keep the bills paid. Effective constructs are essential to business operations. Efficient constructs can make you more profitable. But the alignment of your constructs and workforce is what supports an Internal Franchise.

Organizational structures should serve as corporate guideposts and facilitate the growth of the next generation of leaders. Finally, the culture must become fertile ground that allows the alignment to take place. Every great idea, every new product, every significant initiative will effect change only if it is instituted in a culture that is flexible and adaptive.

Create the Next Generation of Leaders

The COACH mnemonic continues with creating the next generation of leaders. Consider for a minute that your company's growth is in direct relationship to the number of people in your organization. If you are in the services industry, this is most likely the case. To figure out how many team leaders you'll need as your company grows, answer the following leadership math questions:

- What is your projected revenue for the upcoming year?

- What is your targeted revenue per headcount?

- What is your average team size?

As an example, let's look at Stillwater Management Consulting, a fictitious but very typical professional services company. In the calendar year 2010, the total company revenue was $50 million. Since it bills on a time-and-materials schedule (2,000 hours per year) and its average hourly billing rate was $150, its revenue per headcount per year was $300,000. Its average team size is five.

The number of team or project leaders is calculated using the following equation:

(Total revenue / Revenue per headcount per year) / Team size

= Number of team leaders

($50M / $300k) / 5 = 33.

This suggests that Stillwater should have more than thirty team leaders to ensure some modicum of success in its service delivery model.

When Stillwater conducted an operating model exercise, it established that in the calendar year 2015, its revenues would climb to $80 million. Since it was still going to bill on a time-and-materials schedule (2,000 hours per year) and did not forecast a huge increase in its average hourly billing rate ($150 to $170), its revenue per headcount per year would go from $300,000 to $340,000. Stillwater also felt the market was calling for even more flexible consulting teams, so its average team size would shrink to four.

This means that the number of team or project leaders required to meet the company growth projections for the year 2015 would be

(Revenue / Revenue per headcount per year) / Team size

= Number of team leaders

($80M / $340k) / 4 = 59.

Stillwater determined it needed to have fifty-nine team leaders to ensure delivery of the level of service to which their customer base had become accustomed.

In this example, Stillwater forecasts linear growth based on its understanding of future changes in the marketplace. It also suggests that to effectively scale a professional or technical services organization, the key is leadership. Given Stillwater's view of the market, specifically its assessment that all projects would require four people, the only way it will successfully grow and meet its financial objectives is to hire or develop fifty-nine team leaders.

So in general, the development of leadership talent for Stillwater will be key to its success. If its operating model calls for revenue to increase by 50 percent in five years with a similar project profile, the need to create the next generation of leaders becomes critical. Take the leadership math quiz for your organization to help you identify the number of leaders you'll need to grow. Whether your company is growing or holding on for dear life, growing the next generation of leaders will take you to the next level or get you through a tough spot.

Create a Higher Purpose

We wrap up our discussion of leading the Internal Franchise with the final item of the COACH mnemonic, creating a higher purpose.

Creating a higher purpose means creating a reason for being. General George Patton felt his purpose was to lead a great army to victory. That unswerving belief served as motivation to get him out of bed every morning through years of boredom and drudgery in remote army posts all over the world. Like Patton, prospective employees want to be part of something that transcends the routine of daily work. They want to be part of something that has a purpose.

To create a higher purpose, you must envision a future that your employees find compelling. Then you must constantly communicate about that future.

You will have to balance the risk of information overload with the risk of not keeping employees abreast of where the company is going. To keep your communications focused, think of a declaration you can make about your business—a statement intended to create a future to which everyone is committed, even if evidence does not exist to support that future. General Patton's personal declaration was "to lead a great army to victory." It can certainly be argued that in the twenty years leading up to the decisive battles of World War II, he could find very little evidence to support his personal declaration, yet because it served as his ultimate motivator, it eventually became his reality.

As your company develops its higher purpose, ask yourself the following question: if we were to go out of business tomorrow, and nobody was hurt, why would it matter? The employees at King Arthur Flour remind themselves that every day, people across the country count on their flour to make their baking the best it can be.[9] Google's purpose is "to organize the world's information."[10] Amazon's purpose is to be Earth's most customer-centric company."[11] Washington, DC's, Sibley Memorial Hospital's purpose is to "promote wellness, to relieve suffering, and to restore health as swiftly, safely, and humanely as it can be done."[12]

What is the compelling reason your company exists? Do clients rely on your products and services to keep them alive? Would lives be altered or mountains left unclimbed if your company didn't exist?

Remember the story of the two stone masons. For days on end, both were toiling at the physically demanding task of stacking one stone upon another. When the first mason was asked what he was doing, he responded that he was stacking stones and securing them with mortar. But when the other mason was asked the same question, his response was that he was building a cathedral. Who do you think was more personally fulfilled? Which mason would be willing to work late, take on more responsibilities, and groom the next generation of stone masons?

Many of us work in an industry where a higher purpose may be hard to come by. Leaders of companies making mayonnaise, wood pallets, and foam packing peanuts have their work cut out for them! For those leaders, take a lesson from Mac. Mac MacLure is the CEO of RWD, a $190 million technology and training company. He says he always struggled with the emotional aspect of getting buy-in when he wanted to take his company in a new direction. He recognized that working for a training company didn't exactly motivate his employees the same way that working to save lives under the direction of Mother Teresa might have, so he would co-opt the values of his clients.

One of his clients was a major hospital. Mac conveyed to his team that if they built a better training program, they would make this hospital, and potentially many other hospitals, safer and more efficient, resulting in less waiting and more sick people being cared for in a safer manner. Co-opting the values of his clients and showing his team members the ultimate social importance of their work gave them the emotional leverage they needed to connect emotionally with his vision for the future of the company.

Contrast the RWD story with that of Len Moodispaw, CEO of KEYW Corporation, on how he created alignment with his leadership team. He'll tell you his people have a real passion for serving their customers. You see, his customers are the agencies in the United States Intelligence Community, the group chartered to keep us safe and warm. KEYW's leaders long ago bought into the mission, vision, and higher purpose of their customers, so even if parts of their jobs are boring and mundane, when they see a change coming in the customer base, they easily get charged up about it and turn the company in that direction. So whether your company is saving lives or making wood pallets, find a compelling reason for people to come to work every day engaged and fully prepared to contribute to the success of the company.

The Stump Speech

To help develop the thought process of a higher purpose in your organization, encourage each of your next-generation leaders to develop and deliver a stump speech. Project managers, divisional vice presidents, and sales managers should all create and memorize a speech that serves as their declaration of the future. They can use this tool to communicate the corporation's higher purpose to stakeholders, partners, clients, prospects, and employment candidates. Suggest a few simple rules like these:

- Respect the past. Learn from the past. Respect the efforts and accomplishments of your predecessors, but don't dwell on past failures.

- Talk frankly about the reality of the present. Nothing will kill your credibility as a leader quicker than misrepresenting how things currently work.

- Develop an unbounded enthusiasm for the future. Replay videotapes of Martin Luther King's "I Have a Dream" speech or John F. Kennedy's declaration about safely landing a man on the moon. We all want to be a part of a winning team.

Have them develop the speech in the context of their understanding of how the business operates and how they fit into that model. Get them started with something like this:

> Today, I would like to describe the future I see for the
> Consumer Products Division of Sweet Tooth Confections,
> Inc., and the possibilities the future will provide for all
> of us.

This speech becomes a communication tool each leader in the organization will use to inspire a higher purpose in the hearts and minds of every member of the company. Next-generation leaders will use these speeches to align their division or market segment with the higher purpose of the entire company.

The value of the stump speech comes in the effort it takes to create it and the number of times it is repeated. Leaders must be able to unleash versions of their stump speech on a moment's notice. Have them create two or three versions. They should be prepared to deliver a stump speech each time they're in front of more than two employees, each time they meet a customer or a prospective customer, and anytime someone asks them what their company does.

Developing a higher purpose is compelling. It makes you attractive to candidates, clients, prospects, and Wall Street. It makes you excited to get up in the morning. It makes you proud of what you do for a living. It helps you establish your legacy in the business world.

Are you stacking stones or building a cathedral?

Stewards of the Culture

The leadership model of an Internal Franchise suggests we become stewards—stewards of a client, stewards of a process, stewards of an entity that we literally or figuratively own for only a short period, stewards of a corporate culture. Stewardship suggests we care for something during the period of time it is in our charge. It also implies a fiduciary responsibility. This is the position in which most leaders and managers find themselves every day.

You have the opportunity to create additional value in a corporate entity that already has some perceived value. You can effect great change in this corporate entity and add great value to it by creating an environment that is flexible and adaptable and that balances the needs of each of its constituents. You can do this only if your mind-set is to serve your constituents and become a long-term steward over your current environment. Short-term thinking will kill you. Acquiescing to a quarter-by-quarter philosophy meets the needs of only one of your stakeholders.

Your corporate entity already has value. Communicating your purpose casts a wide net for growth and initiative. Growing the next generation of leaders gives the purpose a chance to propagate. Developing teamwork and creating alignment within the organization provides efficiencies for profit and growth.

As you develop an understanding of ownership and stewardship, your ability to lead in an ownership culture will dramatically improve. You'll be able to balance the constant demand for short-term results with the knowledge that a long-term perspective is critical to your business.

Conclusion

Leadership is hard work. Leading in an ownership culture is harder still because it challenges our short-term mind-set and instant-gratification outlook and forces us to take the time to build a company that will stand the tests of time. Leaders in an Internal Franchise must constantly search for every avenue to talk with employees, share information with stakeholders, and manage the constant changes of the market. They have to develop teams that fully appreciate the purpose of the company and align these teams with the higher purpose of the organization. Leaders in an Internal Franchise are asked to check their egos at the door and help develop the next generation of leaders. They are asked to do a great deal; yet when you ask them what they are doing, they answer, "I'm building a cathedral."

Look to the future. Build your business with a purpose higher than making an extra two cents per share next quarter. Seek to inspire a generation of employees to be a part of your version of the information technology revolution.

EPILOGUE

THE PRIMARY GOAL in the drama of business this century has been minimizing the reliance on people. It began with the industrial revolution and the notion of the division of labor; continued with the introduction of productivity-improving technology in the '60s and '70s; progressed through the '80s when revenue growth was achieved through mergers, leveraged buyouts, and acquisitions; and includes the last five to ten years of profit increases fueled primarily through reengineering and rightsizing.

As we enter the second decade of the twenty-first century, many business leaders have discovered they are pursuing the correct goals but with a flawed strategy. The task is no longer a matter of getting the most out of people; it is a matter of people getting the most out of themselves. The company's role in this mind-set shift is to create an environment where employees want to contribute to the goals of the business. The leader's role in this new game is to help all employees "become the best version of themselves."[1] That objective, when transparently and honestly integrated with the formation of an Internal Franchise, allows employees to reach their personal goals while helping the company do the same.

The concepts involved in the creation of Internal Franchises address many of the critical issues facing organizations today. Leaders are always trying to find ways to develop their next generation of leaders. The ability to lead people is critical to the success of any business. Senior executives also believe that increased worker knowledge and skills are important in improving financial results. Understanding the line that exists between the everyday tasks of employees and the financial outcome of the business can separate the winners from the losers. Leaders are also concerned that pay has shifted toward entitlement. They are eager to recast the reward system as part of a larger strategy to motivate and engage employees in a manner that drives improvements to the bottom line. They believe communication is one of the top ways to increase employee productivity and improve financial performance. Finally, business leaders are making a strong connection between financial performance and a strong, empowered corporate culture that shifts employee attitudes and behavior to embrace accountability.

Over the last thirty years, the globalization of the economy has forced companies across the world to reorganize both their structural and financial capital to achieve a competitive edge. But to reach the next level of performance, companies must focus on their human capital—their people.

That's why the creation of Internal Franchises is an idea whose time has come. Internal Franchises directly address the major challenges facing business today, and they represent the last untapped channel of distribution for a company's products and services. Let's review.

Grooming the Next Generation of Leaders

Internal Franchises are all about leadership. In chapter 8, I described the role of the leader as a COACH. The second *C* in

COACH is for "creating the next generation of leaders." Not only do franchise leaders constantly improve their own leadership skills, they diligently work to identify and develop the next generation of leaders. Franchise leaders know that the future of their company depends on leadership. They act as stewards of their company as they develop next-generation leaders.

Growing of Knowledge, Skills, and Abilities

Like a democracy, an Internal Franchise depends on an educated constituency. The growth of employee knowledge begins with defining the operating model as described in chapter 3. By modeling the business along the customer, financial, operating parameter, and core process dimensions, the company leadership can build consensus on how the business works and earns money. The operating model establishes a framework to teach all employees in the company how they impact business performance.

Teaching people how the business works is one of the principles and values in the strong, empowered culture. ("Teach" is the first *T* in the TRUST mnemonic introduced in chapter 5.) When you hire employees, look for their ability to learn your operating model, to teach your operating model, and to improve your operating model. View mistakes as tuition payments—valuable opportunities to create a learning organization.

Paying for Performance

We discussed compensation and reward in both chapters 5 and 6. Reward is the *R* in the TRUST mnemonic.

In an Internal Franchise, employees have a stake in the outcome. Their reward is tied to the performance of the business and their contribution to that performance. Internal Franchise leaders develop compensation programs that motivate appropriate behaviors like stewardship and ownership, and they ensure that all employees understand how they are measured. Then, the leaders apply these measurements consistently to everyone in the organization. Appropriate, clear, and consistent reward systems are a powerful way to motivate and engage employees in a manner that drives improvements to the bottom line and achieves pay for performance.

Communicating

The first *C* in the COACH mnemonic (discussed in chapter 8) is "communication." Internal Franchise leaders constantly communicate about the customer, the company, and the future. They know that what they say has a profound impact on the behavior of their employees and on their perceived leadership abilities. Communication skills are at a premium and are reinforced as important in empowered cultures.

Creating an Empowered Workforce

The heart of an Internal Franchise is the culture of ownership. An ownership culture is a corporate culture that embraces the principles and values of the entrepreneur. Chapter 5 introduced the TRUST mnemonic. TRUST describes the basic values shared by everyone in the Internal Franchise organization; it is the value proposition offered to employees.

Embracing TRUST means that you believe in teaching everyone how the business works. Leaders believe in rewarding employees based on their contribution to the company's performance and unconditionally support them so that true and effective empowerment fills the organization. Leaders share information so that everyone is informed, and they make and keep commitments.

As an Internal Franchise takes hold, the organization experiences initiative, accountability, team spirit, and customer focus. These are the signs of success for an Internal Franchise. And as you discovered in chapter 8, leadership, communication, and creating a higher purpose are equally important in an Internal Franchise.

TRUST, initiative, accountability, team spirit, customer focus, communication, leadership, empowerment, and purpose are the shared values of an Internal Franchise. Ensuring that everyone in your organization embraces these values by making them part of your culture is a powerful performance-enhancing strategy!

NOTES

Introduction

1. Congressional Budget Office, *Budget Report: H.R. 5140 [110th]: Economic Stimulus Act of 2008*, February 11, 2008.
2. International Franchise Association, *Economic Impact of Franchised Businesses* (Washington, DC: IFA, February 2004).
3. Roger L. Martin, *The Design of Business: Why Design Thinking Is the Next Competitive Advantage* (Boston, Harvard Business School Press, 2009).
4. Bill Breen, chapter 1, "The Business of Design," *Fast Company*, April 1, 2005.

Chapter 1

1. "Pierre Foods, Inc. Emerges from Bankruptcy, Names Food Industry Veteran William Toler Chief Executive Officer," *VendingMarketWatch*, December 15, 2008; and "Pierre Foods Files for Chapter 11 Bankruptcy," *Reuters*, July 15, 2008.
2. James Kouzes and Barry Posner, *The Leadership Challenge* (San Francisco: Jossey-Bass, 2002).
3. *WorkUSA—Weathering the Storm: A Study of Employee Attitudes and Opinion*, Watson Wyatt, 2002, http://www.watsonwyatt.com/research/printable.asp?id=w-557.
4. Peter Marshall, Senate chaplain, prayer offered at the opening of the session, April 18, 1947, *Prayers Offered by the Chaplain, the Rev. Peter Marshall, D.D., at the Opening of the Daily Sessions of the Senate of the United States during the Eightieth and Eighty-First Congress, 1947–1948*, Senate Doc. 86 (1949), 20.
5. Malcolm Gladwell, "Rice Paddies and Math Tests," chapter 8 in *Outliers: The Story of Success* (New York: Little Brown and Company, 2008).

Chapter 2

1. *Webster's New International Dictionary*, 3d ed., s.v. "culture."
2. Justice Potter Stewart, Concurring Opinion, *Jacobellis v. Ohio*, 378 U.S. 184 (1964).
3. Max DePree, "Watercarriers," in chapter 5 in *Leadership Jazz* (New York: Doubleday, 1992), 65–75.
4. Barrie Bergman, interview by author, Annapolis, MD, February 25, 2010.
5. Mark Gordon, interview by author, Baltimore, MD, February 17, 2010.
6. John Kotter and James Heskett, *Corporate Culture and Performance* (New York: Free Press, 1992), 15–57.
7. Ibid.
8. *BusinessWeek*, "100 Best Global Brands," http://www.businessweek.com/interactive_reports/best_global_brands_2009.html.
9. CNNMoney.com, "100 Best Places to Work for 2010," *Fortune*, http://money.cnn.com/magazines/fortune/bestcompanies/2010/snapshots/1.html.
10. Christina Breda Antoniades, "Best Places to Work 2010," *Baltimore Magazine*, February 2010.

Chapter 3

1. Wikipedia, s.v. "long tail," http://en.wikipedia.org/wiki/Long_Tail.
2. Laurens Maclure, interview by author, Baltimore, MD, February 7, 2008.
3. Robert G. Hagstrom, *The Warren Buffett Portfolio: Mastering the Power of the Focus Investment Strategy* (New York: John Wiley and Sons, 1999), 1–19.

Chapter 4

1. Zig Ziglar, "Zig Ziglar quotes," ThinkExist.com, http://thinkexist.com/quotes/Zig_Ziglar/.
2. Jimmy Buffett, "Changes in Latitudes Changes in Attitudes," *Changes in Latitudes Changes in Attitudes*, MCA Record Label, 1990.
3. Rodd Wagner and James K. Harter, *12: The Elements of Great Managing* (New York: Gallup Press, 2006), 205.
4. Ibid., 31–49.
5. Mark Ehrnstein, interview by author, Annapolis, MD, February 11, 2010.
6. Patrick Lencioni, *The Five Temptations of a CEO* (San Francisco: Jossey-Bass, 1998).
7. Bruce Ballengee, interview by author, Annapolis, MD, April 8, 2010.
8. Southwest Airlines Co., "Southwest Airlines Fact Sheet," May 23, 2010, www.southwest.com/about_swa/press/factsheet.html.

Chapter 5

1. "Labor Force Statistics from the Current Population Survey," last modified September 30, 2010, http://data.bls.gov/PDQ/servlet/SurveyOutputServlet?data_tool=latest_numbers&series_id=LNS 14000000.
2. Bill Toler, interview by author, Annapolis, MD, March 18, 2010.
3. Alfred E. Kahn, "The Tyranny of Small Decisions: Market Failures, Imperfections, and the Limits of Economics," *Kyklos* 19, no. 1 (1966): 23–47.
4. Garrett Hardin, "The Tragedy of the Commons," *Science* 162, (1968): 1243–1248.
5. Ken Blanchard, John P. Carlos, and Alan Randolph, *The 3 Keys to Empowerment* (San Francisco: Berrett-Koehler, 2001).
6. The World Bank. *World Development Report 1994: Infrastructure for Development* (New York: Oxford University Press, 1994).

Chapter 6

1. Daniel H. Pink, *Drive: The Surprising Truth about What Motivates Us* (New York: Riverhead Books, 2009).
2. Malcolm Gladwell, *Outliers: The Story of Success* (New York: Little Brown and Company, 2008).
3. Bruce Ballengee, interview by author, Annapolis, MD, March 11, 2010.
4. Ken Blanchard, Jim Ballard, and Fred Finch, *Customer Mania! It's Never Too Late to Build a Customer-Focused Company* (New York: Free Press, 2004), 125.
5. Foundation for Enterprise Development, *The Entrepreneur's Guide to Equity Compensation* (La Jolla, CA: Foundation for Enterprise Development, 2002), 11.
6. Corey Rosen, interview by author, Annapolis, MD, February 17, 2010.
7. Interview with subject March 19, 2010.

Chapter 7

1. Max DePree, *Leadership Is an Art* (New York: Dell, 1989), 45–51.
2. Stephen Covey, *Principle-Centered Leadership* (New York: Free Press, 1992), 86–93.
3. Bruce Ballengee, interview by author, Annapolis, MD, February 20, 2010.

Chapter 8

1. Niccolo Machiavelli, "Concerning New Principalities Which Are Acquired by One's Own Arms and Ability," chapter 6 in *The Prince* (New York: Alfred A. Knopf, 1992).

2. "Thomas Jefferson on Politics and Government," University of Virginia, accessed September 30, 2010, http://etext.virginia.edu/jefferson/quotations/jeff0200.htm.

3. Craig McIntosh, interview by author, Boston, MA, March 26, 2010.

4. Sarah McGinley-Smith, interview by author, Annapolis, MD, February 10, 2010.

5. Ken Blanchard and Michael O'Connor, *Managing by Values* (San Francisco, Berrett-Koehler 1996).

6. Nick Morgan, *Trust Me: Four Steps to Authenticity and Charisma* (San Francisco: Jossey-Bass, 2009).

7. *Webster New Collegiate Dictionary*, 1982, s.v. "courage."

8. Ken Blanchard, Susan Fowler, and Lawrence Hawkins, *Self Leadership and the One Minute Manager: Increasing Effectiveness through Situational Self Leadership* (New York: William Morrow, 2005).

9. King Arthur Flour, "About the King Arthur Flour Company," http://www.kingarthurflour.com/about/ (accessed October 12, 2010).

10. Google, "Company Overview," http://www.google.com/corporate/ (accessed October 12, 2010).

11. Amazon.com, "Amazon Investor Relations," http://phx.corporate-ir.net/phoenix.zhtml?c=97664&p=irol-irhome (accessed October 12, 2010).

12. Sibley Memorial Hospital, "About Sibley Memorial Hospital," http://www.sibley.org/general_info/about_sibley_memorial_hospital.aspx (accessed October 12, 2010).

Epilogue

1. Mathew Kelly, *The Dream Manager* (New York: Hyperion, 2007).

INDEX

ACKNOWLEDGMENTS

THE VERY NOTION that one person's name goes on the cover of a book is a bit misleading. All books are team efforts, and this is no exception. The content for this book began to take shape in 1990 when Bob Blonchek, Dan Roche, Ed Calabrese, Luke Garwood, Brian Jachimski, and I began to dream up our first company, Rapid Systems Solutions. We all grew up in the Booz Allen Hamilton culture, and we were convinced we could change the world if we just concentrated on culture and leadership.

Time passed, we sold that company, and Bob Blonchek and I wrote *Act Like an Owner*. We thought we were on the path to being the next Ken Blanchard, and although that dream has shifted over the years, I still feel as though I can change the world though leadership and culture. I've been fortunate to lean on Bob's insight into how businesses operate, and many of the mnemonics used in this book are attributed to Bob's keen sense of keeping things simple. Bob continues to shape his part of the world as the CEO of Razoron.

I later became CEO of CTX Corporation and had the great fortune to work with leaders like Kevin Phillips, Tracy

Graves-Stevens, Dave Horvath, and Mark Longworth. All of these leaders challenged the notion that a culture of ownership could be a differentiator. Their challenges forged many of the practices in this book, and their willing participation in my sandbox will always be appreciated.

In later leadership roles at Canal Bridge Consulting and Conquest, the basic premise that an Internal Franchise and an ownership culture could produce real business results was tested again and passed with flying colors. I thank Susan Stalick of Canal Bridge and Norm Snyder and his leadership team at Conquest for allowing me to lead their companies using the tools and techniques outlined in this book.

After operating companies for many years, I continued to adjust and modify the concepts of an Internal Franchise and an ownership culture in consulting assignments, workshops, and seminars. I would like to thank those who attended my workshops and seminars as well as each of my corporate clients I have had the pleasure of working with over the last six years, including Leo Fox and Matt Wilmoth of Tenacity, Jeanne Kimmich and Kathleen Lally of KSSI, Phil Sahady of Chevo Consulting, Kris Kurtenback of Collaborative Communications, Ray Schwemmer and his team at CollabraSpace, Moira Mattingly and Jeff Leco at Summit Solutions, David Walker of Pangia, Mike Grier of Mosaic, Terri Thomas and her team at BRTRC, and Wayne Beekman and Cary Toor of InfoConcepts.

An element of bringing this book to life was a series of interviews I conducted in 2008 and 2010. Sarah McGinley-Smith, Craig McIntosh, Bruce Ballengee, Mark Gordon, Corey Rosen, Bill Toler, Bob Corlett, Barrie Bergman, Mark Ehrnstein, Mac MacLure, Brad Antle, Rob Baruch, Virginia Callahan, Don Charlton, Gus Cicala, Bob Coleman, John McBeth, Paul Silber, Stan Sloan, and Josh Linker—all leaders in their industries—were willing participants in the interview process, and I thank them very much.

The logistics of bringing a book to market often go unnoticed. I would like to thank Sharon Goldinger, Beverly Butterfield, Mayapriya Long, and Katie Hartlove for their talent and professionalism. I've learned that nothing gets done without Sharon's drive and leadership.

Finally, I would like to thank my family. The life of a husband and father is not always compatible with that of an author, speaker, and consultant, but I am blessed to have a very supportive wife in Denise and three very loving children in Jack, Liam, and Lily. Thank you.

ABOUT THE AUTHOR

MARTIN O'NEILL has spent much of the last twenty-five years operating companies, consulting with senior executives, and writing and researching topics of leadership and culture. As a business operator, he has led start-ups, guided takeovers, steered turnarounds, and managed in private and public corporations. As a consultant, he has worked with CEOs and leadership teams with the goal of building long-term business value. He is currently a principal with Corsum Consulting. Martin is a frequent speaker and consultant on leadership, corporate culture, strategic planning, and building enterprise value and is the coauthor of *Act Like an Owner* (Wiley) and author of *Building Business Value* (Third Bridge Press). He holds a number of board-level positions and sits on the Business Advisory Board for the University of Maryland Baltimore County Tech Center. Martin lives on the Magothy River in Maryland with his wife, Denise, and their three children, Jack, Liam, and Lily.